Reading Success Series

12 Nonfiction Selections

Anthology 1

Passageways®

Series

Dale Lyle,
Project Editor

Lisa Greenleaf Gollihue,
Designer & Illustrator

Susan Hawk,
Photo Researcher
& Illustrator

Leslie Alfred McGrath,
Illustrator

___

**GARE THOMPSON
ASSOCIATES, Inc.,**
Writers

FOR THE STUDENT

This reading book has 12 interesting nonfiction selections. These are the kinds of selections that you might see in school books, in library books, in magazines, and in other kinds of books.

Each selection is followed by 18 multiple-choice questions that give you practice with key reading strategies. Each selection also has 3 Explorations in Writing questions that invite you to write about what you have read.

PHOTO CREDITS:

Front Cover ©2001 ArtToday.com

Pages 5–9, 16, 19, 45, 48–50, 54, 55, 57–60, 66–67, 70, 86, 106–109, 116–118, 120 ©2001 ArtToday.com

Pages 17, 18 Western History/Genealogy Department, Denver Public Library

Pages 24, 25 Courtesy of Lisa Greenleaf Gollihue

Page 64 Digital Vision

Page 68 National Archives and Administration, NWDNS-165-FF-2F-15, Electronic Record, Still Pictures Branch, National Archives at College Park, College Park, MD

Page 69 Library of Congress, Prints and Photographs Division, FSA-OWL Collection, LC-USF33-01696, LC-USF33-01695

Page 69 National Archives and Administration, NRE-79-PS(SB)(PHO)-2341, Electronic Record, NARA's Central Plain Region, Kansas City, MO

Page 74 Robert W. Kelly/TimePix

Page 84 Roger Job/Allsport

Pages 87, 89 AP/Wide World Photos

Page 88 USA Curling Photo Courtesy of Rick Patzke

Page 104 Library of Congress, Prints and Photographs Division, LC-USZ62-122612

Pages 104–110 Background/Courtesy of Lisa Greenleaf Gollihue

Page 110 Western History/Genealogy Department, Denver Public Library

Pages 114, 115, 119 Courtesy of The RV Collection and Lisa Greenleaf Gollihue

Pages 114–120 Background/Courtesy of The RV Collection and Lisa Greenleaf Gollihue

Page 118 Amori/Haga Library

ILLUSTRATION CREDITS:

Pages 4, 65, 74, 76–79, 84, 108 Susan Hawk

Pages 10, 14, 15, 26–30, 34–40, 44–50, 56, 57, 85–90 Lisa Greenleaf Gollihue

Pages 94–98, 100 Leslie Alfred McGrath

TABLE OF CONTENTS

Wolf!

Getting Started

What do you know about wolves? Some people think that wolves are bad animals. What do you think? Read this selection to learn more about the fascinating wolf.

Wolves and Their Relatives

Wolves have fascinated people for a long time. There are many legends and stories about wolves. Some legends say that wolves are kind and wise. But some stories say that wolves are fierce and cunning. What are wolves really like?

The animal that most closely resembles the wolf is the dog. Few people, however, would call the wolf "man's best friend," as the dog is called. To many, the wolf is man's worst enemy. The diagram above shows some ways in which wolves and dogs are similar and different.

As you can see, dogs and wolves share many characteristics. And many people think that wolves look like dogs. Some say that wolves look like German shepherds; others say they look like Alaskan huskies. There's a good reason for people to think that wolves look like dogs. Wolves are related to dogs! The wolf's closest relatives are dogs, coyotes, jackals, and dingos (wild dogs that live in Australia).

Comparing Dogs and Wolves

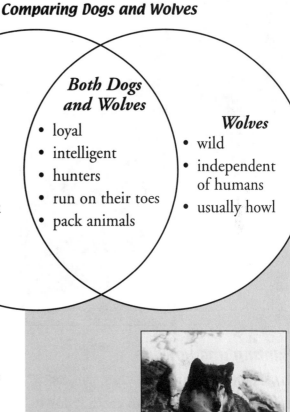

Dogs
- pets
- dependent on humans
- usually bark

Both Dogs and Wolves
- loyal
- intelligent
- hunters
- run on their toes
- pack animals

Wolves
- wild
- independent of humans
- usually howl

Alaskan Husky

German Shepherd

Wolf!

Hunting and Howling

Wolves are hunters. They will eat almost anything they can catch. Mostly, wolves eat small game, but they also prey on larger animals, such as moose and sheep. Sometimes wolves hunt near where people live, and they may kill livestock. As a result, many farmers think of the wolf as their enemy.

Wolves have characteristics that make them good hunters. They are strong animals. Adult wolves can weigh up to 175 pounds. Some adult wolves stretch up to 6 feet from the tip of their nose to the end of their tail. Male wolves are usually larger than females. Most wolves have thick fur that offers good protection against rain and snow. The fur works like a raincoat as water runs off it.

Wolves can run for miles without tiring. They have strong muscles and long legs. When they are chasing large animals, they are like marathon runners, keeping up the chase until they catch their prey. Like dogs, wolves run on their toes. This lets them take long strides. Wolves can run so fast they sometimes look like they are gliding.

Like lions and other hunting animals, wolves have long pointed teeth called canines. Wolves use their canines to grab hold of their prey. They use the small teeth in front of the canines to pick meat off bones. Wolves also have two long teeth that work like scissors to cut the meat off bones.

Strong teeth and powerful bodies make wolves good hunters of large animals. And wolves also have excellent hearing. Like bats and dolphins, wolves can hear things that humans cannot hear. Wolves' fine hearing helps them locate mice and other small animals. Wolves can actually hear mice squeaking and moving beneath logs and snow. Some scientists believe that wolves hunt small prey by using their sense of hearing more than their sense of smell or sight.

A wolf usually hunts alone for small prey, such as mice, ducks, and fish. But for larger prey, such as moose, elk, and deer, wolves generally hunt in packs. It would be too dangerous for a lone wolf to hunt a large animal. Some moose, for example, weigh up to one thousand pounds and stand over six feet tall. When a wolf pack finds a moose, the wolves circle it and try to bring it to a standstill. The wolves work as a team to kill the moose, and then they share the meat. They sometimes howl to call other wolves to share the food.

Howling is a major form of communication for wolves. In calm air, wolves' howls can be heard from many miles away. Wolves howl for various reasons. They may howl to give notice of a kill, to warn of danger, to protect territory, or to locate one another when they have become separated in snowstorms or for other reasons. Often, wolves seem to howl just for the fun of it.

Pack Life

Wolves' lives are centered around the pack. Each wolf pack has a male and a female leader, whom we call the alpha male and the alpha female. The alphas are usually the largest and strongest wolves in the pack. Next there is the beta male and beta female. The beta wolves are not as strong as the alphas, but they are stronger and larger than the other wolves in the pack. Each of the other wolves in the pack has its own place in the order, too. This order helps prevent fighting in the pack. If wolves do begin to fight, the wolf that is lower in the order will often give up before the fight actually starts. This lower wolf will assume a submissive position. It will roll on its back, flatten its ears, and put its tail between its legs. The other wolf will then stop the fight.

Wolves live in dens. When babies, or pups, are about to be born, wolves will either dig a new den or find a fox den or a beaver lodge. If food is scarce, only the pack leaders will mate and have pups.

Most wolves have litters of three pups. Wolf pups are born in the spring. They look like dog puppies and weigh about one pound at birth. They cannot see. The pups' mother stays close to them while others in the pack bring food to her. After two weeks, the pups open their eyes and begin to walk. All the members of the pack help care for the pups. The pups grow quickly. They play at hunting to learn the skills they will need to survive when they are grown. By summer, they look like adult wolves. In the fall, they join in hunts. By winter, they are almost grown. When they are about two years old, some stay with the pack, while others leave to find another pack and to mate. Some will start a pack of their own.

Wolf!

Different Kinds of Wolves

Most wolves belong to the same species, or group: *Canis lupus. Canis* means "dog" and *lupus* means "wolf." But different wolves have different characteristics. Here are three different kinds of wolves for you to compare.

North American Gray Wolf

height: up to about 38 inches

length: up to about 80 inches*

weight: up to about 130 pounds

color: black, gray, brown, white

mate: for life

prey: moose, elk, rabbits, mice

home: upper part of the United States, Canada

North American Red Wolf

height: up to about 16 inches

length: up to about 65 inches*

weight: up to about 90 pounds

color: cinnamon red, brown, buff; with black, red, or tan markings

mate: for life; sometimes mate with coyotes

prey: raccoon, rabbits, birds, small rodents

home: southern areas of the United States but have almost disappeared

Arctic Wolf

height: up to about 31 inches

length: up to about 60 inches*

weight: up to about 175 pounds

color: white, gray, black, red

mate: for life

prey: caribou, musk ox, arctic hare, lemmings

home: frozen tundra of the Arctic

*Length is measured from tip of nose to end of tail.

Wolf!

Wolves Past and Present

Long ago, wolves roamed throughout much of the Northern Hemisphere. They were able to live across this wide area because they could adapt to different climates and conditions. Over time, however, humans have killed most of the wolves. We have trapped them for their fur. We have hunted them to protect livestock. We have taken over their natural environments, forcing them into places where they cannot easily survive. And we have poisoned them with chemicals we use for farming. Only small numbers of wolves remain. And they live mostly in areas where few people live.

But many people have started working to help wolves. Some people provide information about wolves and how they live. This information helps other people see that wolves are not necessarily bad animals.

Other people breed wolves safely and then release them into the wild. These wolves are tracked by radio signal to monitor their progress. Some people don't like this, though. Farmers, for example, often protest when wolves are released into the wild. They are afraid that the wolves will leave the wild areas and start to prey on their sheep and cattle.

It's not only farmers who still think of wolves as dangerous animals. Other people do, too. The question of the true nature of wolves is yet to be resolved.

Wolf!

Finding Main Idea and Details

The main idea is the most important idea. The details are the pieces of information that tell more about the main idea.

1. What is the selection mostly about?
   - Ⓐ wolves
   - Ⓑ red wolves
   - Ⓒ gray wolves
   - Ⓓ wolves and dogs

2. What is a dingo?
   - Ⓐ a wild dog from Borneo
   - Ⓑ a wild cat from Peru
   - Ⓒ a wild wolf from Alaska
   - Ⓓ a wild dog from Australia

3. Which detail is not mentioned in the selection?
   - Ⓐ The North American gray wolf mates for life.
   - Ⓑ A wolf usually has a litter of three pups.
   - Ⓒ Fossils of red wolves are 750,000 years old.
   - Ⓓ The arctic wolf weighs up to 175 pounds.

Finding Word Meaning in Context

Use context clues to find the meaning of a new word. Context clues are words in a sentence that help you figure out the meaning of the new word.

4. On page 5, the word *cunning* means
   - Ⓐ "playful."
   - Ⓑ "helpful."
   - Ⓒ "shy."
   - Ⓓ "tricky."

5. Look at page 7. Something at a *standstill* is
   - Ⓐ not moving.
   - Ⓑ moving quickly.
   - Ⓒ moving slowly.
   - Ⓓ running around in circles.

6. Look at page 8. A wolf in a *submissive* position wants to
   - Ⓐ win.
   - Ⓑ fight.
   - Ⓒ yield.
   - Ⓓ howl.

Wolf!

Recognizing Cause and Effect

When one thing causes another thing to happen, it is called cause and effect. The cause is the reason why something happens. The effect is what happens.

7. Wolf packs have an order so that members of the pack will not
   - Ⓐ howl.
   - Ⓑ eat.
   - Ⓒ mate.
   - Ⓓ fight.

8. Alpha wolves lead the pack because these wolves are the
   - Ⓐ youngest.
   - Ⓑ oldest.
   - Ⓒ largest and strongest.
   - Ⓓ smallest and fastest.

9. Which of these is not a reason for the reduced number of wolves?
   - Ⓐ People have monitored their progress in the wild.
   - Ⓑ People have hunted them to protect livestock.
   - Ⓒ People have trapped them for their fur.
   - Ⓓ People have taken over their natural environments.

Comparing and Contrasting

Comparing is finding how two or more things are alike. Contrasting is finding how two or more things are different.

10. Dogs and wolves both
    - Ⓐ run on their toes.
    - Ⓑ run on their heels.
    - Ⓒ depend on humans.
    - Ⓓ live only in the wild.

11. Wolves, bats, and dolphins share a special sense of
    - Ⓐ smell.
    - Ⓑ taste.
    - Ⓒ sight.
    - Ⓓ sound.

12. On page 6, a wolf's fur is compared to
    - Ⓐ a snowsuit.
    - Ⓑ a raincoat.
    - Ⓒ a hat.
    - Ⓓ a rug.

Wolf!

Understanding Sequence

Sequence is the order in which things are done or events happen.

13. Before wolves have pups, they
    Ⓐ fight for pack leadership.
    Ⓑ move into a den.
    Ⓒ chase away older pups.
    Ⓓ kill a large animal.

14. If wolf pups leave the pack, they do so when they are two
    Ⓐ years old.
    Ⓑ months old.
    Ⓒ weeks old.
    Ⓓ days old.

15. The boxes show how wolves hunt a moose.

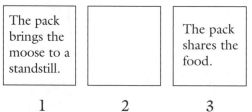

The pack brings the moose to a standstill.		The pack shares the food.
1	2	3

Which of these belongs in box 2?
    Ⓐ The wolves howl to call other wolves.
    Ⓑ The pack chases the moose.
    Ⓒ The pack finds the moose.
    Ⓓ The pack kills the moose.

Drawing Conclusions

Drawing conclusions can help you figure out things that are not written in a selection. To draw a conclusion, think about the facts. Then think about what you know in your own life.

16. If a lone wolf spotted a moose, the wolf would most likely
    Ⓐ not attack.
    Ⓑ attack.
    Ⓒ shake with fear.
    Ⓓ hide.

17. The author of this selection probably feels that wolves
    Ⓐ should be trapped.
    Ⓑ should be hunted.
    Ⓒ are bad animals.
    Ⓓ are not bad animals.

18. Which of these is the wolf's worst enemy?
    Ⓐ people
    Ⓑ moose
    Ⓒ dogs
    Ⓓ sheep

Explorations in Writing

Go to page 124.

THE WILD WEST

Getting Started

What do you think the Wild West was like? Do cowboys, horses, buffalo, and sharpshooters come to mind? Well, that's what "Buffalo Bill" Cody presented in his Wild West Show. Read this selection. Meet Buffalo Bill and some other people who made the Wild West Show the most fascinating show of its time.

COME AND SEE

BUFFALO BILL

WILD WEST SHOW

THE BEST SHOWING

Long ago, most people didn't know much about the West. In the early 1800s, few people traveled west of the Mississippi River. Some thought that the land west of the Mississippi was a vast desert. This area was called the Great American Desert. No one wanted to live there.

Then two explorers went west. They were Meriwether Lewis and William Clark. With their Native American guide, Sacagawea, they traveled all over the West. They found rivers. They found new kinds of plants. They saw buffalo and other animals that no one had ever seen before. Suddenly the West became a wonderful land. It became the land of adventure. Visitors to the West told others about the rich farmland there. People began to move to the West. They sent letters home telling about this new and exciting place. People back home wanted to learn more about the West. They wanted to know more about the people who lived there. But not everyone could travel to the West. How could people learn about this amazing place?

One man had a solution. He knew he could make a lot of money by bringing the West back East. This man was "Buffalo Bill" Cody. He created the Wild West Show.

Meet "Buffalo Bill" Cody

William F. Cody was born in Iowa in 1846. He was the middle child in his family. He was also the only male child to live to adulthood. As a child, Bill worked hard. He loved the outdoors. At the age of eleven, Bill herded cattle. Later, he worked on a wagon train. Next, he became a fur trapper. Then he tried his hand at gold mining. In 1860, he joined the pony express. The pony express was a system of riders who delivered mail. It was hard and dangerous work. Bill Cody loved it.

Shortly after the Civil War, Cody became a scout. At that time, workers were building the railroad across the West. Cody hunted buffalo for the workers to eat. He did this so well the workers began to call him "Buffalo Bill." The name stuck. Cody was proud of the name. As time passed, Buffalo Bill's legend grew. People sang songs about him. They wrote books about him. His picture appeared in newspapers. People wanted to meet this famous man from the Wild West. Buffalo Bill was about to find a new way to make money.

The Wild West Show

In 1872, Bill Cody appeared on stage. He was in a play called *Scouts of the Prairie*. He was not much of an actor. But he was a great showman. All he had to do was be himself. The audiences loved him. They found him charming and handsome. They would listen to him as he told stories about his adventures in the Wild West. The play was a huge success.

Cody decided to form his own touring group. He toured with a show called *Scout of the Plains*. For a time he worked with two old friends and fellow scouts, "Texas Jack" Omohundro and "Wild Bill" Hickok. His friends left the tour. Cody kept going. And people came to see him. They listened and watched. They felt as though they were in the Wild West.

But the plays were not enough for Buffalo Bill. In 1883, he created Buffalo Bill's Wild West Show. It was an outdoor spectacle. Some people compared it to the shows of the ancient Romans. The Wild West Show had a cast of hundreds. It also had live buffalo, elk, cattle, and other animals. And it had real cowboys. They rode broncos, roped cattle, and displayed other skills. Two of the most famous people in the show were Annie Oakley and Sitting Bull.

THE WILD WEST SHOW

Meet Annie Oakley

Buffalo Bill had many good sharpshooters in his show. But the most famous was Annie Oakley. Annie was born Phoebe Ann Mozee. She was born in Ohio on August 13, 1860. Annie learned to shoot at an early age. By the time she was twelve, she could hit a moving quail. With Annie around, her family always had food to eat.

Annie's reputation as a "sure shot" began to spread. People were amazed that the young girl was such a good shot. One day, a shooting act came to her town. Soon a contest was set up between Annie and Frank Butler, a shooter in the act. Butler was one of the best sharpshooters in the country. But Annie beat him. That was fine with Butler though. In time, the two married. Butler told people that he lost a shooting contest but gained a wife. Soon the two were touring with shows. Annie used the name Annie Oakley.

Annie Oakley became famous. Buffalo Bill heard about her and came to see her. He asked her to join his show. In 1884, she did. She had many famous tricks. Annie Oakley was called "Little Sure Shot" because she was only five feet tall. Oakley toured with the Wild West Show for twenty-five years. She had many fans. One fan was Queen Victoria of England. Another fan was Sitting Bull. This famous Sioux Indian chief admired Oakley's skills and called her "daughter."

MEET SITTING BULL

Sitting Bull was born in the Grand River region of what is now South Dakota. The exact year of his birth is not known, but it is believed to be 1831. As a child, Sitting Bull had a nickname that meant "slow." He never hurried, and he always worked with care.

Sitting Bull killed his first buffalo at ten. At fourteen, he joined his first war party. Sitting Bull soon became known as a strong and fearless leader. Around 1867, Sitting Bull became the first chief of the entire Sioux nation. White settlers moving to the West sometimes crossed Native American hunting grounds. The settlers and the Native Americans often fought. Then the United States government and the Native Americans signed a peace treaty. Sitting Bull did not sign the treaty.

Part of the peace treaty had promised that the Black Hills would remain in the hands of the Sioux. This was important to the Sioux. They considered these lands sacred. But then gold was discovered in the Black Hills. Soon gold seekers were camping on Sioux land. Native Americans and the United States Army began to fight each other. They fought a major battle at Little Big Horn. Sitting Bull joined other Native American armies to defeat General Custer. All the white soldiers were killed. Sitting Bull went to Canada. After a harsh winter, Sitting Bull returned. He was put in prison for two years and then released.

Buffalo Bill admired Sitting Bull. He asked Sitting Bull to join his Wild West Show. Many people wanted to see Sitting Bull. Sitting Bull agreed to do it for no more than one year. He agreed to do it only because he needed the money to help his people. After touring with the show, Sitting Bull returned to his people on the reservation. During the time that Sitting Bull was with the show, he became friends with Annie Oakley. The two remained friends for life.

Buffalo Bill's Wild West Show was a huge success. The show toured Europe. It performed before royalty. Buffalo Bill became a millionaire. Some said that Buffalo Bill was the most famous man in the world. Little boys wanted to grow up to be like him. He had fans all over the world. By 1900, the show had traveled thousands of miles. But Buffalo Bill was getting tired. He decided

to retire. He thought he would retire after the show played at the World Exposition in Paris in 1900.

Things did not work out, though. Buffalo Bill was a trusting man. He was too trusting. He had loaned money to many people. He put money into businesses that failed. People took advantage of him. Eventually, he was penniless. But worse than that, he was tricked into selling his show. He was the star of the show but no longer the owner. Tired, "Buffalo Bill" Cody died in 1917. He was buried on top of Look Mountain near Denver, Colorado, in the West he loved.

Today many people visit his grave. They can tour places where he lived. They can read about him in books. Buffalo Bill and the Wild West Show live on. The Wild West is almost as fascinating today as it was over 100 years ago.

Finding Main Idea and Details

The main idea is the most important idea. The details are the pieces of information that tell more about the main idea.

1. This selection is mostly about
   - Ⓐ Annie Oakley.
   - Ⓑ Sitting Bull.
   - Ⓒ the Wild West.
   - Ⓓ the Wild West Show.

2. What did the Sioux consider sacred?
   - Ⓐ the Black Hills
   - Ⓑ Canada
   - Ⓒ gold
   - Ⓓ the United States Army

3. Which of these details was not mentioned in the selection?
   - Ⓐ Buffalo Bill died in 1917.
   - Ⓑ Sitting Bull joined Buffalo Bill's Wild West Show.
   - Ⓒ Annie Oakley was fifteen when she joined the Wild West Show.
   - Ⓓ Frank Butler was Annie Oakley's husband.

Finding Word Meaning in Context

Use context clues to find the meaning of a new word. Context clues are words in a sentence that help you figure out the meaning of the new word.

4. On page 15, what is the meaning of the word *solution*?
   - Ⓐ "problem"
   - Ⓑ "answer"
   - Ⓒ "question"
   - Ⓓ "dream"

5. Look at page 17. The word *spectacle* means
   - Ⓐ "a pair of eyeglasses."
   - Ⓑ "a dotted pattern."
   - Ⓒ "a grand show."
   - Ⓓ "a dull play."

6. Look at page 18. A *quail* is a type of
   - Ⓐ river.
   - Ⓑ tree.
   - Ⓒ feather.
   - Ⓓ bird.

Recognizing Cause and Effect

When one thing causes another thing to happen, it is called cause and effect. The cause is the reason why something happens. The effect is what happens.

7. People could take advantage of Buffalo Bill because he was too
   - Ⓐ smart.
   - Ⓑ trusting.
   - Ⓒ mean.
   - Ⓓ silly.

8. Annie Oakley was called "Little Sure Shot" because she was a great shot and she was
   - Ⓐ only five feet tall.
   - Ⓑ over six feet tall.
   - Ⓒ very young.
   - Ⓓ very cheerful.

9. Sitting Bull is most famous for being
   - Ⓐ a wild sharpshooter.
   - Ⓑ a successful cattle herder.
   - Ⓒ a determined Sioux leader.
   - Ⓓ a friendly Sioux leader.

Comparing and Contrasting

Comparing is finding how two or more things are alike. Contrasting is finding how two or more things are different.

10. Before the explorations of Lewis and Clark, most people thought the West was
    - Ⓐ a great place to visit.
    - Ⓑ a great place to settle.
    - Ⓒ a foggy swamp.
    - Ⓓ a vast desert.

11. Unlike Sitting Bull, Buffalo Bill
    - Ⓐ liked being in shows.
    - Ⓑ never wanted to be in shows.
    - Ⓒ was a good horseman.
    - Ⓓ knew Annie Oakley.

12. Buffalo Bill, Annie Oakley, and Sitting Bull were all
    - Ⓐ wealthy.
    - Ⓑ poor.
    - Ⓒ famous.
    - Ⓓ unknown.

THE WILD WEST SHOW

Understanding Sequence

Sequence is the order in which things are done or events happen.

13. Bill Cody's first job was
    - Ⓐ herding cattle.
    - Ⓑ driving a wagon train.
    - Ⓒ trapping animals.
    - Ⓓ riding with the pony express.

14. Bill Cody became a scout shortly after
    - Ⓐ the War of 1812.
    - Ⓑ the Revolutionary War.
    - Ⓒ the Civil War.
    - Ⓓ World War I.

15. Which event happened first in Sitting Bull's life?
    - Ⓐ He went to Canada.
    - Ⓑ He joined the Wild West Show.
    - Ⓒ He fought at Little Big Horn.
    - Ⓓ He became chief of the Sioux nation.

Drawing Conclusions

Drawing conclusions can help you figure out things that are not written in a selection. To draw a conclusion, think about the facts. Then think about what you know in your own life.

16. The word that best describes "Buffalo Bill" Cody is
    - Ⓐ suspicious.
    - Ⓑ boring.
    - Ⓒ charming.
    - Ⓓ cheap.

17. Why did Sitting Bull not sign the peace treaty?
    - Ⓐ He didn't trust the United States government.
    - Ⓑ He didn't trust the other Sioux leaders.
    - Ⓒ He didn't know anything about the treaty.
    - Ⓓ He didn't care what happened to the Sioux.

18. The main reason the Wild West Show was successful was that
    - Ⓐ people were bored by the West.
    - Ⓑ people were fascinated by the West.
    - Ⓒ there were lots of buffalo in the show.
    - Ⓓ there were no other shows to see.

Explorations in Writing

Go to page 124.

TIDE POOLS

Getting Started

Imagine that you're at the shore. The tide has just gone out, and you're looking into one of the pools the ocean has left behind. What do you see in this tide pool? Tide pools are home to many interesting creatures. Find out about some of these creatures in this selection.

What Are Tide Pools?

Oceans cover two-thirds of the earth. The oceans are filled with fascinating creatures. It's not always easy to learn about them, though. Oceans are enormous and very deep. One way to find out about ocean life, though, is to study tide pools.

You can find tide pools by walking along the rocky shore of the ocean. Tide pools are the pools of ocean water caught between the rocks. These pools are left behind when the tide goes out. Tide pools come in all sizes. Some tide pools are big enough for people to swim in. Others are as small as puddles. Each tide pool gets bigger as the tide comes in. Then it gets smaller as the tide goes out.

Tide pools are home to dozens of different animals and plants. Yet a tide pool is not an easy place in which to live. Most living things are happiest in an environment that changes very little. But tide pools change constantly. The ocean waters rise and fall about twice a day. Waves pound against the rocks, and winds blow. The sun beats down. When it rains, the pools may fill with fresh water. Birds and other animals sometimes try to eat the creatures in the tide pool.

The Changing Conditions in Tide Pools

At high tide, a tide pool is suddenly flooded with seawater. This incoming tide brings oxygen and food to the animals and plants living in the pool. The tide also cleans out wastes.

When the tide goes out, everything changes. The sun warms the water left in the tide pool. Warm water holds less oxygen than cold water. Some small tide pools begin to dry up. Many of the creatures are no longer covered by water at all. Some use parts of their own body as protection. Others hide under rocks or seaweed to keep from drying out.

All the animals that live in tide pools have adapted to rapid change. This means that they have found ways of dealing with the changing conditions in the tide pool.

Observing Tide Pools

It's easiest to study the life in a tide pool when the tide is out. You will see that some tide pool animals look like stones. Some look like plants. Some move very slowly or not at all. Others move so quickly you can hardly see them. The biggest animals in a tide pool are smaller than your hand. The smallest animals are so tiny that you would only be able to see them with a microscope.

Bladder Wrack

Sugar Kelp

Sea Lettuce

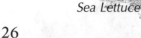

TIDE POOLS

Some Animals That Live in Tide Pools

Periwinkles Periwinkles are some of the first animals you might see in a tide pool. Periwinkles are a type of snail. They spend much of their time high on the rocks around a tide pool. When the tide is in, periwinkles eat tiny plants called algae. The periwinkles scrape the algae off the rocks with their rough tongues. Their tongues are like sandpaper. They scrape so hard that the rocks sometimes get worn down!

Periwinkles get wet for only a short time each day. But they can live for quite a while out of water. When they need to, periwinkles can take water into their shells and close themselves inside. Then they stick to the rocks and wait for the tide to come in again.

Barnacles Other animals also hold onto the rocks in a tide pool. They hold on to avoid being washed away or tossed around by incoming waves. One of these animals is the barnacle. Barnacles are crustaceans. They have an exoskeleton, a hard outer skeleton that surrounds and protects them.

When barnacles are very young, they swim around. Then one day they pick a spot on a rock and cement themselves in place. They make a hard, white outer shell and never move again. Their cement is so strong that even after they die, their shell stays on the rock.

Barnacles

Periwinkles

At low tide, you can hear barnacles clicking tightly shut while they are still full of water. They keep the water inside their shell while the tide is out. When the tide comes back in again, the barnacles open up their shell. Then they stick out their fanlike feet and use them to pull in tiny plants and animals, which they eat.

TIDE POOLS

Crabs Crabs also live in tide pools. Crabs come in a variety of colors and sizes. They scurry across a tide pool, eating almost anything they can find. They are scavengers, which means they eat dead plants and animals. Scavengers do something vital for a tide pool. They clean up all the waste and keep the tide pool clean.

Crabs, like barnacles, are crustaceans. They have a hard exoskeleton that protects them. As crabs grow larger, they molt, or shed, their exoskeleton. They grow a new, bigger one underneath the old one. Crabs also have antennae. The antennae are located on the top of the crab's head. The antennae help the crab feel its way around in the dark.

Crabs have big front claws, called pincers. They use them for grabbing food, walking, digging, and fighting. Even the smallest crab can give a painful pinch. The velvet crab uses its pincers to scare its enemies. It has sharp spikes at the end of its pincers. If the velvet crab is threatened, it rears up and waves its pincers around. This makes the crab look bigger and scarier than it really is.

Crab

Sometimes during a fight, a crab will lose a claw. Usually, a new claw will grow back to replace the lost claw after the crab has molted.

Hermit crabs are different from other kinds of crabs. These little crabs have no hard shell to protect their soft body. So they live in empty snail shells. As hermit crabs grow, they move into bigger empty shells. Sometimes, hermit crabs fight each other for a shell.

Hermit Crab

TIDE POOLS

Sea Anemones   When the tide is out, you might see some rubbery-looking bumps attached to the rocks in the tide pool. These bumps are anemones (uh NEM uh neez). They are meat-eating animals. When the tide comes in, the anemones open up. Then they look like flowers. But the "flower petals" are actually stinging tentacles. An anemone waits for prey to swim by. It stings the prey with its tentacles. Then it pulls the prey into its mouth.

Anemones have soft, jelly-like bodies. They have one big foot with a suction cup on it. They use the cup to hold on tightly to rocks so waves can't knock them off. Once in a while, an anemone might move to a new spot. It attaches itself there with its big foot.

Hermit crabs and anemones often live together. A small anemone may attach itself to a hermit crab's shell. When one eats, the other gets the leftovers. Sometimes a hermit crab will even bring along its anemone when it changes shells.

Sea Anemones

Sea Stars When the tide is out, sea stars—also called starfish—hide under rocks. They cluster together along the floor of a tide pool. Sea stars have flat bodies, and most have five arms. This makes them look like stars. If a sea star loses an arm, it can grow another one in its place. And a whole new animal can sometimes grow from a broken-off arm!

Sea Stars

A sea star has many rows of little tube feet along the underside of each arm. Each tube foot has a sucker on it. This helps the sea star hold onto the rocks. A sea star also uses these strong tube feet for walking. The tube feet are full of fluid. Muscles pump the fluid in and out of the feet to move them up and down.

When the tide rolls back in, sea stars come out to search for food. They can't swim, so they walk around slowly. Any one of a sea star's arms can lead the way. Sea stars are hunters. They eat shelled creatures, such as clams, mussels, and snails.

A sea star uses its arms to pull apart a shell and expose the animal inside. The sea star then inserts its own stomach into the shell of its prey. The sea star's stomach digests the animal inside the shell.

Take a Closer Look at Tide Pools

Lots of other plants and animals also live in tide pools. The next time you're near the ocean, wait until the tide goes out. Take a closer look. Maybe you'll see some of the animals you've just read about, and more.

TIDE POOLS

Finding Main Idea and Details

The main idea is the most important idea. The details are the pieces of information that tell more about the main idea.

1. Which detail was not mentioned in the selection?
   - (A) Hermit crabs live in empty shells.
   - (B) Crabs have big front claws, called pincers.
   - (C) Sea anemones have no skeleton.
   - (D) Sea stars have tube feet.

2. Which tide pool animals have very rough tongues?
   - (A) sea anemones
   - (B) velvet crabs
   - (C) periwinkles
   - (D) sea stars

3. Barnacles are protected by
   - (A) a hard outer skeleton.
   - (B) a hard inner skeleton.
   - (C) tube feet.
   - (D) stinging tentacles.

Finding Word Meaning in Context

Use context clues to find the meaning of a new word. Context clues are words in a sentence that help you figure out the meaning of the new word.

4. On page 28, the word *vital* means
   - (A) "messy."
   - (B) "noisy."
   - (C) "necessary."
   - (D) "unimportant."

5. Look at page 29. *Tentacles* are parts of
   - (A) an animal's body.
   - (B) an animal's house.
   - (C) a tide pool.
   - (D) a tide pool flower.

6. On page 30, the word *digests* relates to
   - (A) cooking food.
   - (B) breaking down food.
   - (C) writing about food.
   - (D) throwing away food.

 TIDE POOLS

Recognizing Cause and Effect

When one thing causes another thing to happen, it is called cause and effect. The cause is the reason why something happens. The effect is what happens.

7. The ability to hold on tightly keeps tide pool animals from being
   - Ⓐ seen.
   - Ⓑ eaten.
   - Ⓒ dried up.
   - Ⓓ washed away.

8. What would not usually happen in a tide pool when the tide was out?
   - Ⓐ The anemones would look like flowers.
   - Ⓑ The anemones would look like rubbery bumps.
   - Ⓒ The periwinkles would be closed inside their shell.
   - Ⓓ The sea stars would be hiding under rocks.

9. Barnacles click their shell shut in order to
   - Ⓐ digest their prey.
   - Ⓑ frighten their enemies.
   - Ⓒ keep water inside their shell.
   - Ⓓ keep water out of their shell.

Comparing and Contrasting

Comparing is finding how two or more things are alike. Contrasting is finding how two or more things are different.

10. Hermit crabs are different from other kinds of crabs because they
    - Ⓐ have their own hard shell.
    - Ⓑ don't have their own hard shell.
    - Ⓒ have claws.
    - Ⓓ are scavengers.

11. The anemone's tentacles are compared to
    - Ⓐ feathers.
    - Ⓑ fans.
    - Ⓒ flower petals.
    - Ⓓ worms.

12. Crabs and sea stars are both able to
    - Ⓐ regrow body parts.
    - Ⓑ kill prey with their tentacles.
    - Ⓒ grow exoskeletons.
    - Ⓓ molt.

Understanding Sequence

Sequence is the order in which things are done or events happen.

13. When the tide comes in, most creatures in a tide pool
    - Ⓐ close their shells.
    - Ⓑ swim away.
    - Ⓒ look for shelter.
    - Ⓓ look for food.

14. As a hermit crab gets bigger, it
    - Ⓐ moves to a bigger shell.
    - Ⓑ grows a hard shell.
    - Ⓒ molts its old shell.
    - Ⓓ finds a bigger anemone.

15. To get to its prey, a sea star first
    - Ⓐ stings the animal.
    - Ⓑ pinches the animal.
    - Ⓒ pulls the animal's shell apart.
    - Ⓓ smashes the animal's shell.

Drawing Conclusions

Drawing conclusions can help you figure out things that are not written in a selection. To draw a conclusion, think about the facts. Then think about what you know in your own life.

16. Which word best describes most tide pool animals?
    - Ⓐ adaptable
    - Ⓑ scary
    - Ⓒ friendly
    - Ⓓ colorful

17. You can tell that the author thinks that studying tide pools is
    - Ⓐ boring.
    - Ⓑ valuable.
    - Ⓒ for children only.
    - Ⓓ for scientists only.

18. When visiting a tide pool, people should
    - Ⓐ walk in, sit down, and feel at home.
    - Ⓒ gather and take home samples of the animals.
    - Ⓑ pick up and observe each type of animal.
    - Ⓓ observe the animals without disturbing them.

Explorations in Writing

Go to page 124.

TIDE POOLS

GROWING UP IN ANCIENT GREECE

GETTING STARTED

How would you like going to school seven days a week from dawn to dusk? Or how would you like not being allowed to go to school at all? If you had grown up in ancient Greece, you might have had one of these experiences. Read this selection to find out more about growing up in ancient Greece.

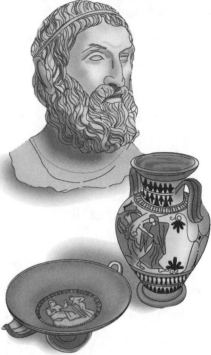

Greece is a land of mountains, islands, and seas. Much of the country is surrounded by water. The sun shines most of the time. Summers are hot and dry. Winters are mild.

Long ago a rich and powerful civilization grew up in Greece. It lasted from about 2000 B.C. to 200 B.C. Its peak, or high time, came between 500 B.C. and 400 B.C.

Ancient Greece was made up of many small city-states. Each city-state had a central city that was surrounded by farmland. The city-states were cut off from one another because of high mountains and rough seas. Each separate city-state developed its own laws and way of life. But most ancient Greeks made their living by farming, fishing, or trading goods.

The ancient Greeks left behind many beautiful works of art, great buildings, and everyday items. These things tell us about their way of life. The ancient Greeks also had great literature, language, ideas, and ways of thinking that are still important today. Young people in ancient Greece grew up in a rich and exciting time.

Early Childhood

When a baby boy was born in ancient Greece, the family hung an olive branch outside their house. If the baby was a girl, they hung a strip of woolen cloth. The family held a special ceremony about a week after the baby's birth. The parents gave the baby a name then. Families did not usually have many children.

Boys and girls under the age of six or seven lived at home. They played together. Their mothers cared for them and taught them. Boys wore few clothes around the house. Girls wore a simple tunic—a short, loose dress. Many children wore a string of charms to protect them from bad luck and illness.

Play

Children in ancient Greece played with some of the same toys that children play with today. Babies had rattles, animal figures, dolls, doll-sized furniture, and pots and pans. Older children played with tops, kites, and yo-yos. They rode on seesaws and swings. Some children had pets such as dogs, geese, weasels, and turtles. Dogs or goats pulled children around in little carts. Parents sang lullabies to their babies. They told their children tales about animals, ghosts, and heroes.

GROWING UP IN ANCIENT GREECE

Family Life

Most families in ancient Greece lived in small, simple houses. These houses were made of dried mud bricks. Roofs were flat and covered with clay tiles. The main rooms were built around an open-air courtyard. Only the family used the courtyard, which could not be seen from the street. The courtyard usually faced south to catch the sun. Because the weather was usually warm, a family spent a lot of time in their courtyard. Children played there. Women did their cooking, spinning, and weaving there.

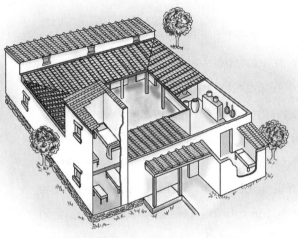

A Typical House in Ancient Greece

Indoors, the kitchen and bathroom were probably next to each other to help keep the bathroom warm. Chamber pots were used instead of toilets. There was no running water. Women washed at home from a large pot or fountain. Men went to public baths to wash. They also met friends and relaxed at the baths.

Greek houses were simply furnished. Families had a few wooden chairs and simple tables. Family members stored things in chests, baskets, and boxes. They rested and slept on couches. They hung colorful hangings on the walls. Sometimes, people lit small oil lamps in the evenings. But most people probably went to bed when the sun went down.

Men and women lived in different parts of the house. Men often entertained friends in their rooms. Women gathered in their rooms to work, visit with friends, and be with their children. Here they made bed covers and clothing for the family. Wealthy women supervised slaves who cooked and cleaned. Poor women had to do this work themselves. Most women seldom left the house.

School

As adults, Greek men had to be able to read notices and write laws. They had to sing and dance at festivals. So Greek boys from wealthy families went to school from age seven to fifteen. Boys from less-wealthy families did not stay in school as long. The families paid the fees for school. The city, however, paid the fees for boys whose fathers had died for their country.

At school, boys learned reading, writing, and mathematics. They memorized poetry. They learned how to dance and play an instrument. The school day went from dawn to dusk with no weekends or holidays off. The only breaks were during festivals.

When a boy was learning to read and write, he used a stylus and a wooden board covered in wax. A stylus was a sharp rod, shaped something like a pen. The boy used the sharp end of the stylus to write on the wax. He used

the broad part of the stylus to smooth out any mistakes. Later the boy would write with ink. The ink came in solid blocks. It had to be mixed with water before it was used.

Household servants often went to school with Greek boys. A servant's job was to watch over a boy's progress. If the boy did not do his work or if he got into trouble, the servant punished him. The boy would sit on a stool before the teacher. The servant watched over the boy from the back of the classroom.

Girls in ancient Greece did not go to school. Girls from wealthy families learned what they could from their mothers or from educated household slaves. Some girls learned to read. All girls learned to cook and look after the household. Girls lived at home until they married.

Work

Children from poor families had to work from a very early age. If their parents were farmers, they might help plant and harvest. Even very little children could scare birds away from the crops.

Training the Body

The ancient Greeks believed in training the body as well as the mind. Beginning at age twelve, boys learned boxing, wrestling, and running. They played ball games. Boys ran races and competed in the long jump and in boxing and wrestling matches. Sporting skills were important because they would help boys become good soldiers as adults.

In some city-states, boys as young as twelve went to live like soldiers. They slept in the open and went barefoot. They were taught how to use weapons and how to fight. Sometimes the boys weren't fed enough. They had to find their own food. They were practicing living like soldiers during war.

Ancient Greeks regularly held public sporting festivals. The games at Olympia were the most famous. These Olympic Games were held every four years. Men came from all over Greece to compete. The prize for winning was a wreath of olive leaves. The Olympics are still held today. Now women compete, too. And the athletes come from all over the world.

Sporting skills were important to the ancient Greeks.

Becoming an Adult

At about age twelve, children in ancient Greece were considered grown up. They went through a ceremony that welcomed them to adult life. Boys and girls brought their toys to a special place and left them there. This was a sign that they had left their childhood behind.

Girls got married early, often at the age of thirteen or fourteen. Their husbands were much older, around thirty. The girl's parents arranged the marriage.

The parents of the bride and groom had to agree on the size of the girl's dowry. A dowry was a gift from the bride's family to the groom's family. Sometimes the bride didn't meet her husband until the day of the wedding. A young woman left the protection of her father to live under the protection of her husband. In ancient Greece, the man was the head of the family.

Finding Main Idea and Details

The main idea is the most important idea. The details are the pieces of information that tell more about the main idea.

1. What is the selection mostly about?
   - Ⓐ the Olympics
   - Ⓑ ancient history
   - Ⓒ living in ancient Greece
   - Ⓓ going to school in ancient Greece

2. Which of these details about ancient Greece was not mentioned in the selection?
   - Ⓐ The school day went from dawn to dusk.
   - Ⓑ The ancient Greeks had no way of writing zero.
   - Ⓒ Summers were hot and dry.
   - Ⓓ Children played with tops, kites, and yo-yos.

3. Homes in ancient Greece did not have
   - Ⓐ running water.
   - Ⓑ colorful hangings.
   - Ⓒ kitchens.
   - Ⓓ courtyards.

Finding Word Meaning in Context

Use context clues to find the meaning of a new word. Context clues are words in a sentence that help you figure out the meaning of the new word.

4. Look at page 36. Some people in ancient Greece thought that wearing *charms* would bring them
   - Ⓐ illness.
   - Ⓑ friends.
   - Ⓒ good luck.
   - Ⓓ bad luck.

5. On page 37, the word *seldom* means
   - Ⓐ "always."
   - Ⓑ "not ever."
   - Ⓒ "not often."
   - Ⓓ "often."

6. Look at page 39. When you *compete*, you try to
   - Ⓐ finish something.
   - Ⓑ buy something.
   - Ⓒ stop something.
   - Ⓓ win something.

Recognizing Cause and Effect

When one thing causes another thing to happen, it is called cause and effect. The cause is the reason why something happens. The effect is what happens.

7. One thing that separated the Greek city-states was
   - Ⓐ vast plains.
   - Ⓑ high mountains.
   - Ⓒ thick forests.
   - Ⓓ hot deserts.

8. Families spent a lot of time in their courtyard because
   - Ⓐ the weather was usually warm, and it was nice out in the courtyard.
   - Ⓑ their houses were too cold and crowded.
   - Ⓒ they didn't like their neighbors.
   - Ⓓ they grew crops in the courtyard.

9. Boys in school used the broad end of a stylus to
   - Ⓐ mix ink with water.
   - Ⓑ paint pictures.
   - Ⓒ write on wax.
   - Ⓓ smooth out any mistakes.

Comparing and Contrasting

Comparing is finding how two or more things are alike. Contrasting is finding how two or more things are different.

10. While young girls in ancient Greece were learning at home, young boys were
    - Ⓐ playing games.
    - Ⓑ getting married.
    - Ⓒ going to war.
    - Ⓓ going to school.

11. Unlike wealthy children, poor children went to
    - Ⓐ work.
    - Ⓑ school.
    - Ⓒ the Olympics.
    - Ⓓ other city-states.

12. Unlike today's Olympics, the Olympic Games in ancient Greece
    - Ⓐ were closed to the public.
    - Ⓑ included swimming competitions.
    - Ⓒ had both men and women competing.
    - Ⓓ had only men competing.

Understanding Sequence

Sequence is the order in which things are done or events happen.

13. The boxes tell what girls in ancient Greece did.

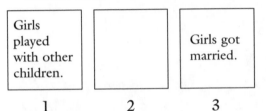

Which of these belongs in box 2?
- Ⓐ Girls learned to write laws.
- Ⓑ Girls went to school.
- Ⓒ Girls learned to care for a household.
- Ⓓ Girls learned games and Olympic sports.

14. Girls and boys left their toys in a special place when they
- Ⓐ became adults.
- Ⓑ went to school.
- Ⓒ went to the courtyard.
- Ⓓ competed in the Olympic Games.

15. Before becoming a soldier, a boy
- Ⓐ learned to play an instrument.
- Ⓑ did household chores.
- Ⓒ got married.
- Ⓓ learned to use weapons.

Drawing Conclusions

Drawing conclusions can help you figure out things that are not written in a selection. To draw a conclusion, think about the facts. Then think about what you know in your own life.

16. Which word best describes the ancient Greek city-states?
- Ⓐ weak
- Ⓑ friendly
- Ⓒ independent
- Ⓓ dependent

17. If you walked down a street in ancient Greece, you probably would not see many
- Ⓐ slaves.
- Ⓑ women and girls.
- Ⓒ soldiers.
- Ⓓ men and boys.

18. Olive leaves and branches probably stood for
- Ⓐ success.
- Ⓑ failure.
- Ⓒ good householding skills.
- Ⓓ good musical skills.

Explorations in Writing

Go to page 125.

Migration

Getting Started

Do you move back and forth from one place to another every year or so? Probably not. But many animals do. Some animals migrate thousands of miles. Read this selection to learn more about migration and some of the animals that migrate.

Many animals migrate, or move back and forth from one place to another. Some migrate to find more food. Some migrate to be in a better climate. Others migrate to be in the best place to give birth and raise their young.

Several different kinds of birds migrate. Each year, they fly to warmer areas in the fall and then return to their homes in the spring.

White Storks These birds migrate each season. In the summer, white storks live in parts of Europe, Asia, and northern Africa. Each year, before it gets cold, the storks fly to northern India, southern China, and other parts of Africa. They spend the winter in these milder climates. Then in the spring they return home. They come back to their original nest to raise their young.

Arctic Terns Terns also migrate. They nest and raise their young around the North Pole and in other northern areas. In late summer, they fly to warmer southern regions. They spend the winter in southern Africa and near the Antarctic. By June, the birds have returned to the North. The arctic tern migrates farther than any other bird. Some may fly as many as 22,000 miles!

White Stork

Arctic Tern

Migration

Gray Whales These large sea animals migrate every year. The whales spend part of the spring, all of the summer, and part of the fall in the northern seas near Russia and Alaska. They find plenty of food there. Gray whales eat tiny shrimp-like animals and other creatures that live in the mud of these northern seas.

In the northern waters, the gray whales eat and grow. They store food energy as blubber. This fat is very important to them. As winter approaches, the whales swim to warmer waters. Many swim south to Baja California. The water is warmer there. But there is less food to eat. So the whales live mainly off their blubber.

Migration

There is a reason that gray whales go to these warm southern waters. They go to mate and give birth. Baby whales, called calves, could not live in the frigid northern seas. They would die. But in the warmer southern waters, the calves drink their mother's milk and grow strong.

When spring comes, the gray whales all return to their feeding grounds in the North. Then the cycle begins again. The whales eat a lot and grow stronger. Then they head south again to give birth. A gray whale may swim as many as 14,000 miles during a year!

Green Sea Turtles These turtles live in warm ocean waters all year long. Every two or three years, the female turtles return to the beach where they once hatched. There they will lay their eggs.

On the home beach, the female digs a nest in the sand. Then she lays her eggs in the nest and covers the eggs with sand. The baby turtles are left to hatch on their own. Once hatched, they dig through the sand to the surface and crawl toward the ocean. Those that make it to the ocean may grow to be adults. The females that make it will repeat the cycle when it is their turn to lay eggs. Somehow, they will find the beach where they were born.

Green Sea Turtles

Salmon

Salmon Like sea turtles, salmon return to where they were born to spawn, or reproduce. But unlike turtles, these fish lay their eggs in water, not on land.

Salmon are born in freshwater streams or lakes. In time, they head for the ocean. There they stay for several years. They eat shrimp, small fish, and other seafood.

When it is time for salmon to spawn, they swim back to where they hatched. They may swim thousands of miles. Many scientists think that salmon use ocean currents, the position of the sun, and a sense of smell to find their way. Salmon often battle dams and rough currents to swim upstream to their home. Once there, they spawn. Many salmon die after they have spawned just once.

Migration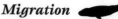

Caribou This type of large deer lives in cold northern lands. Caribou live in huge herds, which number thousands of animals each. In the spring, the caribou move to calving grounds. Here the mothers give birth. The young spring plants in these calving areas provide good food for the caribou. By mid-summer, however, biting bugs often force the caribou to move again. This time they may head toward the coast. There the coastal breezes can blow the insects away. Sometimes caribou even find patches of snow to roll around in to get rid of the insects. In late summer, the caribou head back to their winter feeding grounds.

Caribou

Monarch Butterflies Some insects migrate. Monarch butterflies, for example, cannot survive cold northern winters. The temperature and the length of day tell the butterflies when it is time to leave. As winter approaches, swarms of butterflies flee Canada and the northern United States. Millions of them wing their way to warmer southern spots. There they crowd together on certain kinds of trees, as in this photo.

In spring, the butterflies begin their return trip home. Along the way, females lay eggs on milkweed plants and then die. The young from the eggs turn from caterpillars into butterflies. They continue the long journey north.

For butterflies and other animals, migration can be dangerous. But migrating animals continue to make their long and often dangerous journeys in order to thrive and survive.

Monarch Butterflies

Migration

Finding Main Idea and Details

The main idea is the most important idea. The details are the pieces of information that tell more about the main idea.

1. Pages 46 and 47 are mainly about
   - Ⓐ Baja California.
   - Ⓑ ocean shrimp.
   - Ⓒ gray whales.
   - Ⓓ baby animals.

2. Which of these details was not mentioned in the selection?
   - Ⓐ Swallows migrate.
   - Ⓑ Monarch butterflies lay their eggs on milkweed plants.
   - Ⓒ Many gray whales migrate to Baja California.
   - Ⓓ Arctic terns may fly up to 22,000 miles when they migrate.

3. Which animal often dies after it lays its eggs?
   - Ⓐ the salmon
   - Ⓑ the caribou
   - Ⓒ the green sea turtle
   - Ⓓ the white stork

Finding Word Meaning in Context

Use context clues to find the meaning of a new word. Context clues are words in a sentence that help you figure out the meaning of the new word.

4. Look at page 47. *Frigid* means
   - Ⓐ "blue."
   - Ⓑ "somewhat cool."
   - Ⓒ "extremely cold."
   - Ⓓ "wavy."

5. On page 48, what does the word *cycle* mean?
   - Ⓐ "a series of events that repeats"
   - Ⓑ "a series of events that does not repeat"
   - Ⓒ "a single event"
   - Ⓓ "several unrelated events"

6. On page 50, the word *survive* means
   - Ⓐ "go home to."
   - Ⓑ "run away from."
   - Ⓒ "die."
   - Ⓓ "live through."

Recognizing Cause and Effect

When one thing causes another thing to happen, it is called cause and effect. The cause is the reason why something happens. The effect is what happens.

7. Whales swim to warmer waters to
   Ⓐ find their original home.
   Ⓑ find food.
   Ⓒ add blubber.
   Ⓓ give birth.

8. Scientists think that salmon may use which of the following to find their way home?
   Ⓐ musical sounds
   Ⓑ ocean currents
   Ⓒ stars in the sky
   Ⓓ shoreline scenery

9. Monarch butterflies migrate because they
   Ⓐ cannot live in the cold.
   Ⓑ can live only in the cold.
   Ⓒ want a new home.
   Ⓓ have to cluster on trees.

Comparing and Contrasting

Comparing is finding how two or more things are alike. Contrasting is finding how two or more things are different.

10. The white stork and the arctic tern both migrate
    Ⓐ to lay their eggs.
    Ⓑ to raise their young.
    Ⓒ to be in a warmer climate.
    Ⓓ to be in a drier climate.

11. Unlike sea turtles, salmon
    Ⓐ lay their eggs on land.
    Ⓑ lay their eggs in the water.
    Ⓒ return home to lay their eggs.
    Ⓓ go to a new place each year to lay their eggs.

12. Monarch butterflies travel in swarms; caribou travel
    Ⓐ in herds.
    Ⓑ in schools.
    Ⓒ in pairs.
    Ⓓ singly.

 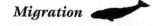

Understanding Sequence

Sequence is the order in which things are done or events happen.

13. The boxes tell about gray whales.

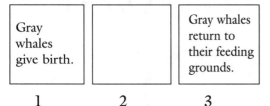

Gray whales give birth.		Gray whales return to their feeding grounds.
1	2	3

Which of these belongs in box 2?

Ⓐ Gray whales swim south.
Ⓑ Gray whales store blubber.
Ⓒ The calves eat shrimp and grow strong.
Ⓓ The calves drink mothers' milk and grow strong.

14. Right after a green sea turtle lays her eggs, she
Ⓐ covers the eggs with sand.
Ⓑ returns to her home beach.
Ⓒ digs a hole in the sand.
Ⓓ guides her young to the ocean.

15. Before salmon return home to spawn, they live for several years in
Ⓐ dams.
Ⓑ the ocean.
Ⓒ freshwater ponds.
Ⓓ freshwater streams.

Drawing Conclusions

Drawing conclusions can help you figure out things that are not written in a selection. To draw a conclusion, think about the facts. Then think about what you know in your own life.

16. Which word best describes salmon that are swimming upstream to spawn?
Ⓐ relaxed
Ⓑ determined
Ⓒ ridiculous
Ⓓ terrified

17. Once hatched, how many baby turtles probably make it to the ocean?
Ⓐ none of them
Ⓑ all of them
Ⓒ some of them but not all of them
Ⓓ all of the males but none of the females

18. How do migrating animals probably find their way back and forth?
Ⓐ They remember past trips.
Ⓑ They are lucky.
Ⓒ Only scientists know for sure.
Ⓓ No one knows for sure.

Go to page 125.

Benjamin Franklin

Getting Started

How much do you know about Benjamin Franklin? Do you know that he was an inventor, a writer, and a statesman? Well, he was all that and more. Read this selection to learn more about this amazing man.

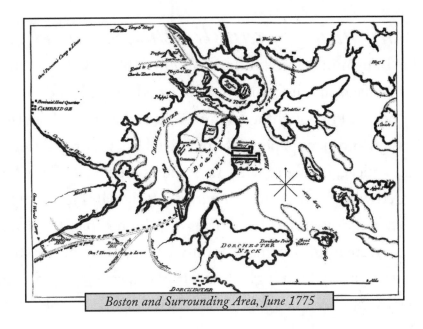

Boston and Surrounding Area, June 1775

Benjamin Franklin as a Boy

Benjamin Franklin was born in Boston, Massachusetts, on January 17, 1706. His parents had seventeen children. Benjamin was one of the youngest. His parents worked hard. They needed all their children to work, too. But they let Benjamin go to school. He went to school for just two years. He did not do very well in school. He was great at reading but not very good at writing. He did badly in math.

Benjamin's father did not want to spend any more money on school for him. School seemed to be a waste of money since Benjamin did not do very well. His father thought that Benjamin should work. When he was ten, Benjamin began to help his father at work. Benjamin's father made candles and soap. Soon Benjamin was making candles, too.

Benjamin Franklin the Learner

But Benjamin wanted to learn. He was like a sponge. He soaked up facts and information. He loved to read, and he read lots of books. He bought as many books as he could. He also read essays and newspapers. He practiced his writing. After he read a piece, he wrote what he remembered of it. Then he compared what he had written with the original. He corrected his mistakes. Sometimes his writing was better than the original!

Soon Benjamin became a good writer. But he didn't stop with just writing. He taught himself math, science, and many languages. He became one of the best-educated people of his day. But how would he earn a living?

. . . the Printer

Benjamin's father knew that Benjamin did not want to be a candle maker. Benjamin wanted to be a sailor. But one of Benjamin's brothers had died at sea. His father did not want Benjamin to be a sailor. His father found him a different job. By the time he was twelve, Benjamin was working for his older brother, James. James was a printer.

Some Printer's Tools

He printed newspapers. Benjamin learned how to become a printer.

Benjamin signed a paper saying he would work for James for nine years. When he was twenty-one, he could leave James. Then he could work on his own. But Benjamin did not want to work for his brother for that long. When Benjamin was seventeen, he left James. He went to Philadelphia, Pennsylvania. He wanted to have his own print shop.

. . . the *Writer*

By 1730, Benjamin Franklin owned his own print shop. For almost forty years, he printed a newspaper called *The Pennsylvania Gazette*. Franklin wrote much of the newspaper himself. He was the first person in America to print a newspaper cartoon. He worked hard. His newspaper sold very well. Soon he became famous.

An Early Printing Press

An Early Print Shop

Franklin also became famous for one book. It was called *Poor Richard's Almanac.* Each year from 1733 to 1758, Franklin wrote and published a new almanac. The almanac included weather predictions, jokes, and poems. It also included many proverbs. People still use these wise sayings of Benjamin Franklin. Here are five of Franklin's proverbs.

- *A penny saved is a penny earned.*
- *Early to bed and early to rise, makes a man healthy, wealthy, and wise.*
- *An ounce of prevention is worth a pound of cure.*
- *A true friend is the best possession.*
- *He that speaks much, is much mistaken.*

. . . the *Improver*

Franklin thought of many different ways to make life better for people. Here are some things he did. Franklin

- *improved mail service in the colonies.*
- *started the first volunteer fire department in the colonies.*
- *helped start the first library in the colonies.*
- *raised money to build a hospital in Philadelphia.*
- *started a program to pave, clean, and light Philadelphia streets.*
- *helped start a school that later became the University of Pennsylvania.*

. . . the *Experimenter*

Franklin also liked to experiment with things. One time he flew a kite during a thunderstorm. The kite had a metal tip. A key was tied to the end of the kite string. During the storm, lightning hit the kite. It traveled down the string and made the key

spark. (Franklin was lucky he was not holding the kite string at that point. The electricity would probably have killed him.) But Franklin did show that lightning is electricity!

. . . the Inventor

Franklin invented the lightning rod. A lightning rod is a metal pole that helps keep buildings safe from lightning. The rod sticks up above the building's roof. The rod leads to a wire. The wire leads to another rod in the ground. If lightning hits the rod on the roof, it travels along the rod, to the wire, and into the ground. Before there were lightning rods, lightning often struck buildings and started fires.

Franklin also invented the rocking chair and a wood-burning stove. His stove could heat rooms better than other kinds of stoves. It is still used today. It is called the Franklin stove. Franklin also invented a type of eyeglasses called bifocals. The lenses of these glasses have two parts. One part helps a person see far away. The other part helps the person see close up.

Ben Franklin and the Franklin Stove

 *Benjamin Franklin*

... the Statesman

Benjamin Franklin was also a statesman. He wrote a plan to join the colonies as one country. And he helped write the Declaration of Independence. This important paper told Great Britain that the colonies were free and why.

Franklin traveled to other countries. He asked them to help the American colonies win their freedom. One country he went to was France. The French people liked him. Crowds followed him through the streets. Poets wrote poems about him. But the French government was not sure it wanted to help the American colonies. It did not think the colonies could win a war against Great Britain. Franklin did not give up. Finally, France agreed to help the colonies.

The Liberty Bell was rung in 1776. It celebrated the Declaration of Independence. The bell is in Philadelphia, where Franklin lived.

The colonies won the war against Great Britain. Franklin worked on the treaty that said the war was over. But Franklin worked on an even more important paper. When he was eighty-one, he helped write the Constitution of the United States. It stated the laws of the new country.

Benjamin Franklin did a lot for people and for his country. He helped the United States become the strong country it is today.

Finding Main Idea
and Details

*The main idea is the most important
idea. The details are the pieces of
information that tell more about
the main idea.*

1. This selection is mostly about
   Benjamin Franklin's
   - Ⓐ inventions.
   - Ⓑ childhood.
   - Ⓒ life.
   - Ⓓ famous sayings.

2. Which of these details was not
   mentioned in the selection?
   - Ⓐ Franklin traveled to England.
   - Ⓑ Franklin traveled to France.
   - Ⓒ Franklin invented a wood-
     burning stove.
   - Ⓓ Franklin was a printer.

3. Where did Benjamin Franklin have
   his print shop?
   - Ⓐ Boston
   - Ⓑ Philadelphia
   - Ⓒ Chicago
   - Ⓓ New York

Finding Word Meaning
in Context

*Use context clues to find the meaning
of a new word. Context clues are words
in a sentence that help you figure out
the meaning of the new word.*

4. On page 56, what is the meaning
   of the word *essays?*
   - Ⓐ "books about mining"
   - Ⓑ "short pieces of writing"
   - Ⓒ "long newspaper articles"
   - Ⓓ "difficult math problems"

5. On page 57, *predictions* tell about
   - Ⓐ the present.
   - Ⓑ the past.
   - Ⓒ the future.
   - Ⓓ forever.

6. On page 58, the word *pave* means
   - Ⓐ "color."
   - Ⓑ "clean."
   - Ⓒ "uncover."
   - Ⓓ "cover."

Recognizing Cause and Effect

When one thing causes another thing to happen, it is called cause and effect. The cause is the reason why something happens. The effect is what happens.

7. Benjamin Franklin went to work when he was ten because he
    Ⓐ   refused to go to school.
    Ⓑ   didn't do well in school.
    Ⓒ   had never been to school.
    Ⓓ   couldn't find a school near his home.

8. Benjamin Franklin's father did not want him to become a sailor because
    Ⓐ   one of Benjamin's brothers had died at sea.
    Ⓑ   one of Benjamin's brothers had run away to sea.
    Ⓒ   no one in the family had ever been to sea.
    Ⓓ   Benjamin was not strong enough to be a sailor.

9. Benjamin Franklin is famous for his
    Ⓐ   successes in battle.
    Ⓑ   national parks.
    Ⓒ   writing and inventions.
    Ⓓ   songs.

Comparing and Contrasting

Comparing is finding how two or more things are alike. Contrasting is finding how two or more things are different.

10. In school, young Benjamin Franklin was good in
    Ⓐ   all of his subjects.
    Ⓑ   none of his subjects.
    Ⓒ   reading but not in math.
    Ⓓ   math but not in reading.

11. Over time, Benjamin Franklin
    Ⓐ   got worse at math.
    Ⓑ   became an expert candle maker.
    Ⓒ   lost interest in writing.
    Ⓓ   improved his writing.

12. As a learner, Benjamin Franklin is compared to
    Ⓐ   a sponge.
    Ⓑ   a dishrag.
    Ⓒ   a book.
    Ⓓ   a candle.

Benjamin Franklin

Understanding Sequence

Sequence is the order in which things are done or events happen.

13. Benjamin Franklin's first job was
    Ⓐ making candles with his father.
    Ⓑ writing *Poor Richard's Almanac*.
    Ⓒ working in his brother's print shop.
    Ⓓ running his own print shop.

14. After he lived in Massachusetts, Franklin moved to
    Ⓐ France.
    Ⓑ Washington, D.C.
    Ⓒ Pennsylvania.
    Ⓓ Great Britain.

15. Franklin worked on the Constitution when he was
    Ⓐ eighteen.
    Ⓑ twenty-one.
    Ⓒ fifty.
    Ⓓ eighty-one.

Drawing Conclusions

Drawing conclusions can help you figure out things that are not written in a selection. To draw a conclusion, think about the facts. Then think about what you know in your own life.

16. Young Benjamin Franklin's parents were
    Ⓐ carefree.
    Ⓑ silly.
    Ⓒ practical.
    Ⓓ cruel.

17. Benjamin Franklin worked for his brother James
    Ⓐ for one year.
    Ⓑ for five years.
    Ⓒ for nine years.
    Ⓓ all his life.

18. Which of these words does not describe Benjamin Franklin?
    Ⓐ timid
    Ⓑ inventive
    Ⓒ determined
    Ⓓ wise

Explorations in Writing

Go to page 126.

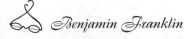
Benjamin Franklin

It's GOLD!

Getting Started

People throughout time have wanted to own gold. Gold has been used as money. It has been made into jewelry and other prized objects. What makes gold so special? Read this selection to find out more about gold.

It's GOLD!

Tin, iron, and lead are useful metals. They are used in tools and other practical objects. Silver is a valued metal. It is used in jewelry and other special items. But the most prized and sought-after metal of all time is gold!

Some Details About Gold

Gold is a dense and heavy metal, yet it is soft. Gold is sometimes mixed with a metal like copper or silver. This makes the gold harder. Gold is yellow in color. It does not lose its luster over time. If you found some very old silver coins, they would be blackened. But if you found some very old gold coins, they would still be bright and shiny. And gold does not rust or flake either, as some other metals do.

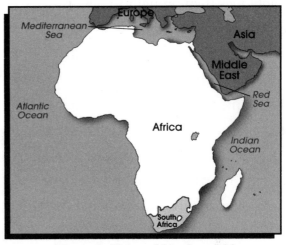

Almost half the gold in the world comes from South Africa.

Gold is found in the earth, and people dig mines to get it out. Some countries that mine gold are the United States, Canada, and Australia. But almost half the gold in the world comes from South Africa, which has vast mines. Miners collect gold from veins in these mines. They seldom find gold nuggets. But once they found a nugget that weighed 12 pounds. One of the largest gold nuggets ever found weighed 195 pounds! It was found in California.

Since ancient times, people have searched for gold. Gold stands for wealth. Gold seekers want to get rich, or richer.

It's GOLD!

Gold in Ancient Times

The Egyptians In ancient times, Egypt was probably the richest gold-producing area. At first, people found gold close to the surface. Later, they dug tunnels in fields and mountains. These tunnels were up to seventy yards long. Workers mined for gold in the tunnels. The gold was then brought to major cities. There jewelers made jewelry and other objects out of the gold. Wealthy people bought these objects.

In Egypt, gold became very valuable. It became a sign of wealth. Egyptian rulers began to use gold dishes and cups every day. They sat on gold thrones and carried gold scepters, or rods. Gold showed their wealth and power.

When rulers in ancient Egypt died, they were buried with many gold objects in their tombs. Over time, robbers found the tombs and stole the gold. The robbers missed at least one tomb, though. In 1922, King Tut's tomb was discovered. In the tomb was a gold coffin. Also in the tomb were gold drinking cups and beautiful gold jewelry. These pieces are now in museums, so many people can view them.

The Greeks and Romans The ancient Greeks and Romans also used gold. The rulers wore gold crowns. Some Greek statues had gold on them, as the statue of Zeus shown below. One Greek ruler, Croesus (KRES suhs), had an enormous amount of gold. He used gold to show his wealth and power. But Croesus also did something special with gold. He minted, or made, the first gold coins. Later the Romans also used gold coins throughout their mighty empire.

This Greek statue of Zeus was made of gold. Notice the size of the statue compared to the people observing it.

It's GOLD!

The Search for Gold

The rulers of old began to keep gold just for themselves. Most other people could not get gold. Gold became very sought after. Some people tried to get gold in unusual ways. People who were called alchemists believed they could turn other metals into gold. They tried using different chemicals and formulas to turn metal into gold. But none of them were able to.

Rulers wanted more gold. They sent explorers out to find it. Spain sent many explorers to the Americas in search of gold. Columbus was searching for gold and spices when he landed in America. Later, Coronado led a search for gold in what is now the southwestern United States. He had heard a legend of the Seven Cities of Gold. He set out to find these fabled cities. He never found them. But he did discover the Grand Canyon.

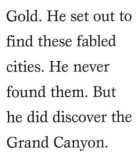

Many of the native people in the Americas at that time mined gold. They used it to make jewelry and art objects. Explorers brought some of these gold objects back to Europe. Later, explorers forced the native people to mine gold for them. Then the explorers sent the gold back to Europe.

Over time, gold became the coin of the land. People began to use gold to pay for goods. Countries needed more gold. So they continued to search for it. Each time someone discovered gold, a gold rush began. People left their homes to rush to the new discovery. They all hoped to strike it rich.

Coronado was searching for the Seven Cities of Gold. He didn't find them. But he did find the Grand Canyon!

 **It's GOLD!**

The California Gold Rush

One major gold rush took place in California. In January of 1848, James Marshall had a work crew on the American River near Sacramento. They were building a sawmill for John Sutter. One morning, Marshall found a few tiny gold nuggets. Word of his discovery spread rapidly. Soon, thousands of prospectors poured into California to search for gold.

A Gold Rush Town

Most of the prospectors panned for gold in rivers. Many hoped to strike it rich. Very few did. Soon, however, gold was discovered in several other places. More people streamed into California. People began to stake claims. Others opened mines. They dug tunnels and found gold. By 1852, California's gold production was $81 million per year.

Life as a prospector was hard. People lived in tents or in the open. It was hot during the day and cold at night. People had little food. They fought over claims.

Prospectors came into town with the day's gold. Often they spent it all on food, supplies, and entertainment. The next day they had to start all over again. Prospectors still dreamed of striking it rich. But the people who made the most money were often the shopkeepers. They sold supplies. Some charged $5 for a pound of sugar and $15 for a shovel. Those were very high prices for that time.

One man who made money by selling supplies was Levi Strauss. He knew that miners needed sturdy pants. So he made the first dungarees. Soon all the miners were buying and wearing his pants. Today people all over the world wear dungarees.

It's GOLD!

Gold was sometimes carried by wagon trains.

A Golden Mystery

In 1853, gold was discovered in Canada. Many miners left California. The California gold rush was over. But gold was still very sought after. As gold became more valuable, there were more and more gold robberies. Thieves robbed trains carrying gold. They robbed banks holding gold. Many robberies were solved. But one robbery is still a mystery.

In 1865, just after the American Civil War, a $100,000 gold shipment disappeared in Georgia. Thieves stole two wagon trains filled with gold.

France had loaned the money to the South. The gold was on its way back to France. While soldiers were waiting for their orders, the gold disappeared. No one knows what happened to the gold. Some say the gold was divided among local people. Others say it was buried in a nearby river. Some say it was buried on a local plantation. Soldiers questioned the local people. But the gold was never found. No one was ever seen spending any gold coins. After heavy rainstorms, however, gold coins were often found on dirt roads near the plantation. Some people believe that the treasure is hidden somewhere near the plantation. People still search. No one has found the gold yet.

 **It's GOLD!**

Gold Today

Gold continues to be a precious metal. Many people wear gold jewelry. They go to museums to view gold objects from ancient times. People and businesses buy and sell gold. Some people buy gold as an investment. They hope that the price of gold will increase. Then they can sell the gold and make money.

Countries still use gold as payment for goods. The United States stores its gold in Fort Knox in Kentucky. In 1936, the government built a special building at Fort Knox for the gold. The gold is stored as gold bars, not coins. The gold is kept in a steel and concrete vault. This underground chamber is sixty feet long and forty feet wide. The walls are two feet thick. Many security devices protect the gold.

Today gold is a symbol of excellence as well as wealth. In competitions, winners are often given gold medals for first place. We use many expressions that show the importance of gold. We say "good as gold," a "golden age," and a "golden child." Gold is still a very special metal.

Gold objects from ancient times are on display in many museums today.

It's GOLD!

Finding Main Idea and Details

The main idea is the most important idea. The details are the pieces of information that tell more about the main idea.

1. Look at page 69. What is this page mostly about?
   - Ⓐ a gold robbery
   - Ⓑ gold in the South
   - Ⓒ shipping gold
   - Ⓓ mining gold

2. Which detail about gold was not mentioned in the selection?
   - Ⓐ Gold is a dense and heavy metal.
   - Ⓑ Fool's gold is a metal that looks like gold.
   - Ⓒ One gold nugget weighed 195 pounds.
   - Ⓓ South Africa produces half the world's gold.

3. The United States stores its gold in
   - Ⓐ Georgia.
   - Ⓑ France.
   - Ⓒ Kentucky.
   - Ⓓ California.

Finding Word Meaning in Context

Use context clues to find the meaning of a new word. Context clues are words in a sentence that help you figure out the meaning of the new word.

4. Look at page 65. *Luster* relates to how a metal
   - Ⓐ feels.
   - Ⓑ sounds.
   - Ⓒ looks.
   - Ⓓ smells.

5. On page 65, *veins* are found
   - Ⓐ in the earth.
   - Ⓑ in an arm.
   - Ⓒ on a leaf.
   - Ⓓ on a roof.

6. Look at page 67. Something that is *fabled* exists mainly
   - Ⓐ in truth.
   - Ⓑ in stories.
   - Ⓒ in museums.
   - Ⓓ on maps.

 **It's GOLD!**

Recognizing Cause and Effect

When one thing causes another thing to happen, it is called cause and effect. The cause is the reason why something happens. The effect is what happens.

7. Gold is sometimes mixed with copper or silver to make the gold
   Ⓐ brighter.
   Ⓑ rougher.
   Ⓒ softer.
   Ⓓ harder.

8. Coronado discovered the Grand Canyon when he was looking for
   Ⓐ the Seven Cities of Gold.
   Ⓑ the California gold fields.
   Ⓒ the West Coast.
   Ⓓ Columbus.

9. People poured into California in the mid-1800s to
   Ⓐ become farmers.
   Ⓑ become shopkeepers.
   Ⓒ search for gold.
   Ⓓ search for silver.

Comparing and Contrasting

Comparing is finding how two or more things are alike. Contrasting is finding how two or more things are different.

10. Unlike gold, silver can
    Ⓐ melt.
    Ⓑ rust.
    Ⓒ turn yellow.
    Ⓓ turn black.

11. The ancient Greeks and Romans both used gold in
    Ⓐ coins.
    Ⓑ scepters.
    Ⓒ tombs.
    Ⓓ first-place medals.

12. Unlike most prospectors during the California gold rush, the shopkeepers
    Ⓐ lost money.
    Ⓑ made money.
    Ⓒ lived in tents.
    Ⓓ wore dungarees.

It's GOLD!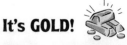

Understanding Sequence

Sequence is the order in which things are done or events happen.

13. The boxes tell about the California gold rush.

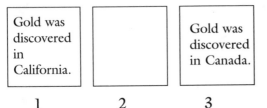

Gold was discovered in California.		Gold was discovered in Canada.
1	2	3

Which of these belongs in box 2?
Ⓐ Many miners left California.
Ⓑ California's gold production reached $81 million a year.
Ⓒ A gold shipment disappeared in Georgia.
Ⓓ The gold rush ended in California.

14. A $100,000 gold shipment disappeared in Georgia in 1865
Ⓐ as the gold was being returned to France.
Ⓑ as the gold was being received from France.
Ⓒ at the beginning of the American Civil War.
Ⓓ in the middle of the American Civil War.

15. The vault at Fort Knox was completed in what year?
Ⓐ 1800
Ⓑ 1836
Ⓒ 1900
Ⓓ 1936

Drawing Conclusions

Drawing conclusions can help you figure out things that are not written in a selection. To draw a conclusion, think about the facts. Then think about what you know in your own life.

16. Which word best describes most of the prospectors in the California gold rush?
Ⓐ smart
Ⓑ friendly
Ⓒ wishful
Ⓓ angry

17. How does owning gold make most people feel?
Ⓐ powerful
Ⓑ healthy
Ⓒ talented
Ⓓ lazy

18. Tourists are probably not allowed inside
Ⓐ museums that house ancient Egyptian jewelry.
Ⓑ the vault at Fort Knox.
Ⓒ the Grand Canyon.
Ⓓ California.

Explorations in Writing

Go to page 126.

It's GOLD!

73

LANGSTON HUGHES

Getting Started

Langston Hughes is a famous American poet who often listened to jazz as he wrote. Through his work, Hughes told what it was like to be African American. Read this selection to find out more about the life and work of Langston Hughes.

LANGSTON HUGHES, *the Original Jazz Poet*

the Original Jazz Poet

∽ *Young Langston* ∽

Langston Hughes was born on February 1, 1902, in Joplin, Missouri. His father had studied to be a lawyer. His mother had gone to college. But life was hard for African Americans in the United States. Langston's father asked to take the test to become a lawyer. He was told he could not because he was African American. Furious, he moved to Mexico, leaving his family behind. Langston was still a baby. Langston's mother worked at many different jobs. She was always trying to find something better.

When Langston was five years old, his mother brought him to the nearest school. It turned out to be for whites only. School officials said Langston should go to the nearest school for African Americans. Langston's mother said no. She went to the school board and won. Langston was the first African American child to go to his elementary school. He had a hard time there. Some teachers and students were mean to him. Sometimes children chased him home and threw stones at him. But he had some friends at school, too.

When Langston was seven, he went to live with his grandmother. She was a widow of about seventy. She was proud and strong and had spent most of her life fighting to help African Americans. She had very little money, so she and young Langston struggled. But she told Langston wonderful stories about African American heroes. She read and talked to him about freedom. She taught Langston to be proud of who he was.

*L*angston's grandmother died when he was twelve. He went to live with family friends for two years. When Langston was fourteen, his eighth grade class had to elect officers. The last officer to be chosen was class poet. No one in the class had ever written a poem. But the students, who were mostly white, believed that black people had natural rhythm. So they elected Langston Hughes class poet. Honored, Langston went home and wrote his first poem, sixteen verses praising his classmates and his teachers. When he read his poem at graduation, everyone cheered! Langston had found his calling.

Langston's mother remarried. He went to live with her and his new stepfather in Cleveland, Ohio. Langston went to high school there. He was good-looking and friendly. He was a good student. He was also a good athlete and a member of the track team. In high school, everyone liked Langston.

Langston had many jobs during high school. He worked at a soda fountain. He worked in a department store. For a while he lived in Chicago, where his mother had moved. She wanted him to quit school and get a full-time job. Langston refused. Instead, he went back to Cleveland to finish high school. He rented a room. He had little money. He couldn't go out to eat. He ate rice and hot dogs in his room every night. He read and studied. And he wrote poems.

LANGSTON HUGHES, *the Original Jazz Poet*

∽ *Hughes Grows Up* ∽

*H*ughes spent the summer after high school visiting his father in Mexico. His father promised to pay for his college education if Hughes became an engineer. But Hughes didn't want to be an engineer. He wanted to be a writer.

Around this time, Hughes wrote his first serious poem. He wrote it quickly on the train to Mexico, crossing the Mississippi River. He called it "The Negro Speaks of Rivers." The poem was published! Hughes was finally a real poet. After this success, he wrote poems often. Usually he wrote them quickly. He believed that poems were like rainbows. They could escape quickly.

To please his father, Hughes finally did go to Columbia University in New York City. He studied engineering. He wasn't happy at school. But he loved New York City. He spent most of his time in Harlem. This was the section of the city where most African Americans lived. Harlem was crowded and lively. Hughes went to the theater to see musicals. He went to clubs to listen to music. He didn't go to classes often. But he did write more poems.

After a year, Hughes dropped out of college. He was twenty-one. He decided that he wanted to make his own decisions about his life from then on.

☙ *Success at Last* ☙

*H*ughes decided to take a job on a ship sailing for Africa. He wanted to see the homeland of all African Americans. Later he took another job on a ship heading for Europe. He arrived in Paris with just a few dollars. He lived in Europe for a year. He worked at odd jobs. He was often hungry. But he saw some of the great sights of Europe. And he continued to write poems. Finally he worked his way home on another ship. He arrived in New York with just a few cents in his pocket.

What was next for young Hughes? He had learned a lot through travel. Now he felt that he had to go to college. But he had no money. He made a few dollars by selling his poems and by winning prizes for his writing. He had become better known. Then his first book of poems, *Weary Blues*, was published in 1926. Success brought Hughes new friends. Friends paid for

him to attend Lincoln University in Pennsylvania. But he went back to Harlem whenever he could.

Harlem had become the center of the arts for African Americans. Artists, writers, and composers produced new works there. Musicians, actors, and singers performed in Harlem. This exciting time was called the Harlem Renaissance, or rebirth of the arts. Hughes became friends with many of these African American artists. One friend introduced him to Charlotte Mason, a rich white woman. Mrs. Mason supported some of the African American artists. She gave them money so that they could do their work. She chose Hughes to be one of these artists. With this money, Hughes was able to write a novel, *Not Without Laughter*. It was published in 1930. He followed it with other novels, stories, poems, and plays.

LANGSTON HUGHES, *the Original Jazz Poet*

❧ *Hard Times* ❧

ℬy this time, the Harlem Renaissance had ended. The Depression had begun. It was a time of great hardship and suffering. Many people lost their jobs. Some lost their homes and didn't have enough to eat.

Hughes had a big decision to make. He had broken his ties with Charlotte Mason and no longer had her support. Times were hard. What could he do to make a living? He had never been able to support himself with just his writing. Even so, he decided that he would become a writer. To support himself, he gave poetry readings at schools, colleges, and universities around the country. He gave readings almost every evening and sometimes on Sunday afternoons. He traveled hundreds of miles every week. At these readings, he also sold copies of his poems and books.

Hughes told his audiences about his childhood and about how he had come to write poetry, and then he read his poems. Many of the poems were about the daily lives of African Americans. Most of Hughes's listeners were African American students. In school, they had read the poetry of white poets only. They were shocked to meet a black poet. Hughes encouraged them to read other African American poets and writers. For the first time, many did.

⚮ *A Jazz Poet* ⚮

*H*ughes always loved to travel. He was curious to see how people in other places lived. During the 1930s he was invited to visit many countries, including Russia, Japan, and China. He also returned to Mexico for a while. He never had much money, but he was used to living hand-to-mouth. Hughes never traveled without his phonograph and his jazz records. He played jazz all over the world.

In 1937 a newspaper asked Hughes to travel to Spain. He was to write about the Spanish Civil War. A number of African Americans were fighting there. Hughes went, and he wrote many stories for the newspaper. He kept writing poetry, too. He called the poems *Letters from Spain*. He wrote while he played jazz music, which he kept loud to cover the sounds of the bombs.

Some people called Hughes the original jazz poet. He wrote poems that included the sounds of jazz. During his poetry readings, he often played jazz in the background.

Hughes continued to write and give readings until the end of his life, but he never made much money. During his lifetime, African American writers were largely ignored. But today Langston Hughes is an honored writer. His works are included in many books of American poetry.

Finding Main Idea and Details

The main idea is the most important idea. The details are the pieces of information that tell more about the main idea.

1. Langston Hughes's grandmother told him stories about
   Ⓐ Columbia University.
   Ⓑ African American heroes.
   Ⓒ ancient Greek heroes.
   Ⓓ his mother and father.

2. Which of these details was not mentioned in the selection?
   Ⓐ Hughes won a Guggenheim Fellowship.
   Ⓑ Hughes was class poet.
   Ⓒ Hughes went to Lincoln University.
   Ⓓ Hughes's father lived in Mexico.

3. Hughes usually wrote poetry
   Ⓐ carelessly.
   Ⓑ painfully.
   Ⓒ quickly.
   Ⓓ slowly.

Finding Word Meaning in Context

Use context clues to find the meaning of a new word. Context clues are words in a sentence that help you figure out the meaning of the new word.

4. On page 76, what is the meaning of the word *calling*?
   Ⓐ "wealth"
   Ⓑ "career"
   Ⓒ "poem"
   Ⓓ "problem"

5. Look at page 79. Someone who is *shocked* is
   Ⓐ angry.
   Ⓑ sad.
   Ⓒ amused.
   Ⓓ surprised.

6. Look at page 80. A *phonograph* is a type of
   Ⓐ song.
   Ⓑ poem.
   Ⓒ machine.
   Ⓓ writing tool.

Recognizing Cause and Effect

When one thing causes another thing to happen, it is called cause and effect. The cause is the reason why something happens. The effect is what happens.

7. Hughes left Columbia University because he
   - Ⓐ wanted to be a writer, not an engineer.
   - Ⓑ wanted to be an engineer, not a writer.
   - Ⓒ ran out of money.
   - Ⓓ did not like New York City.

8. Hughes sailed to Africa because he wanted to
   - Ⓐ leave the noise of Harlem behind.
   - Ⓑ see the homeland of all African Americans.
   - Ⓒ see the beautiful scenery.
   - Ⓓ become a professional sailor.

9. Hughes gave poetry readings because
   - Ⓐ Mrs. Charlotte Mason asked him to.
   - Ⓑ his publisher asked him to.
   - Ⓒ he could earn money and continue to write.
   - Ⓓ he could earn money and no longer have to write.

Comparing and Contrasting

Comparing is finding how two or more things are alike. Contrasting is finding how two or more things are different.

10. Langston's mother and grandmother each had
    - Ⓐ stood up for the rights of African Americans.
    - Ⓑ ignored the rights of African Americans.
    - Ⓒ dedicated her life to making more money.
    - Ⓓ decided it was better to live in Mexico.

11. Some of Langston's elementary school classmates threw stones at him, but his eighth-grade classmates
    - Ⓐ elected him class president.
    - Ⓑ elected him class poet.
    - Ⓒ ignored him.
    - Ⓓ chased him home.

12. Hughes compared poems to
    - Ⓐ stars.
    - Ⓑ puzzles.
    - Ⓒ snowstorms.
    - Ⓓ rainbows.

Understanding Sequence

Sequence is the order in which things are done or events happen.

13. The boxes show some events in Hughes's life.

Hughes lived with his grand-mother.	Hughes lived in Europe for a year.	
1	2	3

Which of these belongs in box 3?
- Ⓐ Hughes was elected class poet.
- Ⓑ Hughes wrote "The Negro Speaks of Rivers."
- Ⓒ Hughes attended Columbia University.
- Ⓓ Hughes attended Lincoln University.

14. Hughes wrote his very first poem
- Ⓐ while at Columbia University.
- Ⓑ on his way to visit his father in Mexico.
- Ⓒ while living with his grandmother.
- Ⓓ when he was elected class poet.

15. Hughes wrote *Not Without Laughter*
- Ⓐ before he wrote *Weary Blues.*
- Ⓑ before he was introduced to Mrs. Charlotte Mason.
- Ⓒ after he was introduced to Mrs. Charlotte Mason.
- Ⓓ after he wrote *Letters from Spain.*

Drawing Conclusions

Drawing conclusions can help you figure out things that are not written in a selection. To draw a conclusion, think about the facts. Then think about what you know in your own life.

16. Which of these words does not describe Langston Hughes?
- Ⓐ funny
- Ⓑ determined
- Ⓒ curious
- Ⓓ creative

17. Which probably had the most influence on Hughes's poems?
- Ⓐ Mexico
- Ⓑ jazz
- Ⓒ nature
- Ⓓ Paris

18. Throughout most of his life, Langston Hughes valued
- Ⓐ others' opinions more than his own.
- Ⓑ white artists more than black artists.
- Ⓒ money more than art.
- Ⓓ art more than money.

Explorations in Writing

Go to page 127.

THE OLYMPIC GAMES

Then and Now

Getting Started

Have you ever watched the Olympic Games on TV? These games were first held over twenty-five hundred years ago. At that time, people loved to watch skilled athletes compete. And we still do! Read this selection to find out more about the Olympic Games.

The First Olympic Games

The first Olympic Games were held in 776 B.C. in Olympia, Greece. That's where the games got their name. The games were part of a festival that was held every four years. Men came from all over Greece to compete. And as many as forty thousand people came to watch and cheer!

In the beginning, the games had just one race. The runners ran one length of the stadium, about two hundred yards. As the years passed, the Greeks added new sports. For example, boxing, chariot racing, and a five-sport event called the pentathlon became part of the games. The ancient pentathlon included running, jumping, wrestling, throwing the javelin, and throwing the discus. (The javelin is like a spear. The discus is like a wooden plate.)

At one point, the Greeks added an unusual race to the Games. In this race, runners wore metal armor. The armor weighed around fifty pounds. These men had to work hard to run wearing all that metal. They earned their prizes.

The ancient Olympic Games continued until the year A.D. 393. Then a Roman ruler stopped them. There were no games for about fifteen hundred years. In 1896, a man from France decided to start up the games again. His name was Pierre de Coubertin.

The Games Today

In 1896, the Greeks held the first modern Olympics. These summer games were held in Athens, Greece. Athletes from thirteen countries competed in nine sports.

Over time, the Olympic Games grew. By 1996, the 100th anniversary of the games, they were huge. That year the games were held in the United States in Atlanta, Georgia. And 10,000 athletes from 197 countries came to compete! There were now 26 sports in the games.

The Olympic Games today are different from the ancient games. The original games were only a running race. Today's games, however, cover thirty different sports. In ancient Greece, only men competed. Today both men and women compete. In horseback riding, in fact, men and women compete against one another. Long ago, the games were always held in Olympia. Today's games are held every two years in different cities in different parts of the world. And since 1924, there have been both summer and winter games.

One thing hasn't changed over time, though. Everyone admires athletes who compete for their country. Olympic winners are often treated like heroes.

Today there are Senior Olympic Games .

. . . and Special Olympic Games.

The Summer Games

What do boxing, sailing, and table tennis have in common? They are all sports in the Summer Olympic Games. So are diving, swimming, gymnastics, archery, rowing, and shooting, among others. People keep adding sports to the games. Skateboarding is one popular sport that was recently added.

Track and field events are very popular in the Summer Games. These are the running, jumping, and throwing sports. Some Olympic track and field athletes have become famous. Carl Lewis is one of them. Lewis won nine gold medals in track and field! He jumped almost thirty feet in the long jump. That's farther than a cheetah can jump! In recent games, Marion Jones was the first woman to win five medals in track and field. She won three gold and two bronze medals. Just being in the games is an honor. People work hard for years to make it.

Carl Lewis

Some Olympic athletes compete in the modern pentathlon. Pierre de Coubertin, the man who started the modern games, added this event to the games. He had heard a story about a soldier. The soldier had to deliver a message. First, the soldier rode his horse. Then he had to fight the enemy with his sword and gun. When his horse was hurt, he ran through the woods. Finally, he swam across a river. At last, the soldier delivered his message! Similarly, athletes in today's pentathlon ride horses, fence, shoot, run, and swim. Many say the pentathlon is the hardest event in the Summer Games.

The Winter Games

At one time, the Olympic Games were held only in the summer. But people wanted to see winter sports, too. So winter sports were added one by one. First, people built indoor ice rinks. Then figure skaters could compete. Next, ice hockey teams began to play in the games. But people wanted to see other winter sports, too. They wanted to see skiing and bobsledding. These sports had to be played outdoors. The first Winter Olympic Games were held in 1924. They were held in a small mountain village in France.

Curling

Today athletes in the Winter Games still ice skate, bobsled, ski, and play hockey. But they also ski jump and snowboard. And they play a sport called curling. In curling, players slide heavy stones across smooth ice toward a circle.

In 1956, the Winter Games were held at Cortina, in the mountains of Italy. Cortina usually had a lot of snow. But in the winter of 1956, hardly any snow fell. People began to worry that there would be no games that winter. The Italian army came to the rescue. Here's what they did.

- The soldiers drove trucks into the mountains.
- They loaded the trucks with snow from the mountains.
- They drove the trucks down to Cortina.
- They dumped the snow onto the ski slopes. But the weather turned warm. The snow melted!
- The soldiers brought more snow down. This time it did not melt. The Winter Games were held.

Some Famous Olympic Athletes

Olympic athletes have become famous for many reasons. Some have won gold medals. Others have broken records by doing something better than anyone else. And some athletes have become famous for surprising everyone!

Dan Jansen with His Daughter

Dan Jansen became famous for surprising everyone. He was an Olympic speed skater. In the 1988 Winter Games, he was expected to win a gold medal. But right before his first race, he found out that his sister had died. He skated anyway. But he fell down and lost the race. In another race, he fell again. Four years later, Dan Jansen tried again. People were sure that this time he would win. But he lost again. Then, in 1994, Jansen gave himself a last chance at Olympic gold. He had two tries this time. Jansen slipped in the first race. He lost his chance for a medal. Now he had only one last race to skate. When he slipped in this race, everyone thought he was finished. But instead of falling, he kept going. He came around the last turn and crossed the finish line first. The crowd exploded. Dan Jansen had finally won the gold! Everyone cheered as Jansen skated around the rink with his baby daughter in his arms.

Nadia Comaneci

Nadia Comaneci was another famous Olympic athlete. She was a gymnast from the country of Romania. She was fifteen years old when she competed in the 1976 games. Nadia was a tiny girl. She was four feet eleven inches tall. She weighed about eighty-six pounds. That year, Nadia became the first gymnast in the world to score a perfect 10. That is the highest score possible! By the time the Olympics were over, Nadia had gotten a perfect 10 seven times! She took home three gold medals, one silver, and one bronze.

The Flame

Have you ever watched the opening of the Olympics? If you have, you might have seen the Olympic flame being lit. That flame was first lit in Olympia. No matches were used.

Now the Olympic flame is lit every two years in a special ceremony. A woman dressed like a person from ancient Greece holds an unlit torch. She puts it over a special piece of glass called a lens. The lens is shaped like a big cone. When the rays of the sun are caught inside the cone, they get very hot. The hot rays make the torch burst into flame. Then the woman touches her flaming torch to torches held by runners. The runners carry the flame on to other people holding torches. Each torch is used to light the next. This is called the torch relay. In this way, the Olympic flame travels around the world.

When the flame arrives in the city where the Olympics are being held, another ceremony is held. This time, someone uses the relay flame to light a big torch in the stadium. It is a special honor to light the big Olympic torch. Once this torch is lit, the Olympic Games begin.

Here are some amazing Olympic flame facts.

Sometimes the flame travels by plane, train, or boat. Sometimes it travels in more unusual ways. It has traveled by warship and helicopter. It has been shot through the air on a burning arrow. And it has been carried underwater, using a special waterproof torch.

In 1992, there were 10,083 runners who carried the flame from Greece to Spain.

In 1996, for the 100th Anniversary Olympic Games in Atlanta, Georgia, the flame traveled over fifteen thousand miles! It took eighty-four days for the flame to get from Olympia to Atlanta. That was the farthest and longest trip the flame has taken yet.

Finding Main Idea and Details

The main idea is the most important idea. The details are the pieces of information that tell more about the main idea.

1. What is the selection mostly about?
   - Ⓐ the Summer Games
   - Ⓑ the Winter Games
   - Ⓒ the Olympic Games
   - Ⓓ famous Olympic athletes

2. Which of these details was not mentioned in the selection?
   - Ⓐ The first games were held in Olympia, Greece.
   - Ⓑ Tara Lipinski won a gold medal for figure skating.
   - Ⓒ The first Winter Games were held in 1924.
   - Ⓓ The 100th anniversary of the games was in 1996.

3. Which of these did not happen in the ancient Olympics?
   - Ⓐ Women competed in the games.
   - Ⓑ Men competed in races.
   - Ⓒ During one kind of race, men wore armor.
   - Ⓓ A Roman ruler stopped the games in A.D. 393.

Finding Word Meaning in Context

Use context clues to find the meaning of a new word. Context clues are words in a sentence that help you figure out the meaning of the new word.

4. On page 85, what does *festival* mean?
   - Ⓐ "a one-time event"
   - Ⓑ "a special celebration"
   - Ⓒ "dinner time"
   - Ⓓ "an unhappy time"

5. Look at page 87. The word *common* tells about
   - Ⓐ something shared.
   - Ⓑ something separate.
   - Ⓒ a public place.
   - Ⓓ a mark in a sentence.

6. Look at page 89. The word *exploded* means
   - Ⓐ "left."
   - Ⓑ "blew up."
   - Ⓒ "responded in a quiet way."
   - Ⓓ "responded in a noisy way."

Recognizing Cause and Effect

When one thing causes another thing to happen, it is called cause and effect. The cause is the reason why something happens. The effect is what happens.

7. The Olympics got their name from
   - Ⓐ the runners in the first race.
   - Ⓑ the place where the first games were held.
   - Ⓒ the ruler of Greece at the time of the first games.
   - Ⓓ the ruler of Rome at the time of the first games.

8. The Winter Games were started because people
   - Ⓐ wanted to see winter sports.
   - Ⓑ were bored in the winter.
   - Ⓒ were bored with the Summer Games.
   - Ⓓ wanted to visit Cortina.

9. In 1994, no one expected Dan Jansen to win his last race because he
   - Ⓐ had won several earlier races.
   - Ⓑ had slipped in an earlier race.
   - Ⓒ was too slow.
   - Ⓓ was too fast.

Comparing and Contrasting

Comparing is finding how two or more things are alike. Contrasting is finding how two or more things are different.

10. One sport that is part of both the ancient pentathlon and the modern pentathlon is
    - Ⓐ swimming.
    - Ⓑ running.
    - Ⓒ shooting.
    - Ⓓ wrestling.

11. Carl Lewis's jump is compared to the jump of
    - Ⓐ Nadia Comaneci.
    - Ⓑ Pierre de Coubertin.
    - Ⓒ a horse.
    - Ⓓ a cheetah.

12. As in the past, today's Olympic medal winners are thought of as
    - Ⓐ children.
    - Ⓑ heroes.
    - Ⓒ movie stars.
    - Ⓓ fast runners.

Understanding Sequence

Sequence is the order in which things are done or events happen.

13. Which of these sports was most recently added to the Olympics?
    - Ⓐ skateboarding
    - Ⓑ wrestling
    - Ⓒ running
    - Ⓓ discus throwing

14. To prepare for the 1956 winter Olympics, the Italian soldiers first
    - Ⓐ dumped snow onto the ski slopes.
    - Ⓑ loaded trucks with snow.
    - Ⓒ drove trucks into the mountains.
    - Ⓓ replaced the melted snow.

15. The Olympic flame is lit by
    - Ⓐ a gold match.
    - Ⓑ a kitchen match.
    - Ⓒ a huge candle.
    - Ⓓ a lens.

Drawing Conclusions

Drawing conclusions can help you figure out things that are not written in a selection. To draw a conclusion, think about the facts. Then think about what you know in your own life.

16. In horseback riding,
    - Ⓐ men have more skill than women.
    - Ⓑ women have more skill than men.
    - Ⓒ men and women have equal skill.
    - Ⓓ children have more skill than adults.

17. The Winter Games are held in areas that are
    - Ⓐ hilly.
    - Ⓑ flat.
    - Ⓒ sandy.
    - Ⓓ damp.

18. What does the author probably value most about the Olympics?
    - Ⓐ They create competition.
    - Ⓑ They create superstars.
    - Ⓒ They include winter sports.
    - Ⓓ They include athletes from around the world.

Explorations in Writing

Go to page 127.

Women Get the VOTE

Getting Started

Voting for our leaders is one of the special rights that all American citizens have. Not everyone in the United States has always had the right to vote, though. Women, for example, did not win the right to vote until 1920. Read this selection to learn more about how women won the vote.

VOTES FOR WOMEN

Early Voting Laws

Today all United States citizens who are at least eighteen years old have the right to vote. People vote to choose their leaders. They vote on important issues. They vote to help make the laws of their country, state, and town.

Not everyone has always been able to vote, though. Long ago, only a few people in the United States could vote. Only men who owned property could vote. Women, children, and slaves could not vote. Anyone who was not white could not vote. From 1776 until 1787, the laws on voting stayed the same.

In 1787, leaders from each of the states met to plan how the government of the United States would work. These leaders wrote out their plan. It became the Constitution. The Constitution gave each state the right to decide who could vote.

By 1830, the states had decided that all adult white male citizens could vote. Voters no longer needed to own property. But women and people who were not white still could not vote. Some people did not think this was fair.

Early Conditions for Women

When the Constitution was written, many people felt that women should not be allowed to vote. They believed that women needed to be taken care of, either by their fathers or their husbands. They thought that women should only take care of their homes and look after their children.

Most unmarried women lived at home. They were supposed to obey their fathers. Wives were supposed to obey their husbands. A wife belonged to her husband. If a father gave his daughter a house, it became her husband's property once she married. Married women could not own land, buildings, or other property. Everything a wife had, even her clothes, belonged to her husband.

Women often did not go to school past grammar school. Many people thought women did not need an education. These people thought that women should just get married and have children. They believed that women did not belong in the workplace. They felt that women were not strong enough to work. Some even thought women

were not as smart as men. Women could get few jobs. But if a woman did work, the money she made belonged to her husband.

Most women worked hard in the home. Household chores took a long time. They were hard work. Women had no timesaving tools, such as washing machines and vacuum cleaners. Many women were treated like servants.

The Move Toward Independence

Over time, people began to change their minds. Some came to believe that women should be educated. They thought that women should be trained for jobs. More women went to school longer. Many began to earn their own money. As women became more independent, they wanted the same rights as men. They believed that they should be allowed to vote.

By the 1820s, more women were working. Many textile, or cloth, mills had been built in New England. Young women left their homes to work in the mills. They were paid little, and the work was hard. But they were taking care of themselves. Now women also wanted to make decisions about how the country was run.

During the 1800s, many people wanted slavery to end. As some women fought to end slavery, they learned important skills. They learned how to make speeches, organize people, and raise funds. Women began to use these skills to fight for their own right to vote.

A former slave, Sojourner Truth spoke out against slavery and for women's rights.

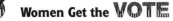

The Fight Continues

In 1848, a group of women held a meeting to discuss the rights of women. The meeting was held in Seneca Falls, New York. The leaders of the meeting were Elizabeth Cady Stanton and Lucretia Mott. These two women had met years earlier at an antislavery meeting.

Together they made an important decision. They decided to start a new organization. Its goal would be to help women win the same rights that men had. The most important right was the right to vote. If women had the vote, they could vote for laws that helped women.

Many people today think that this meeting was the start of the fight for equal rights for women. But at the time, many people did not think much of the meeting. In fact, many newspapers made fun of the meeting. But this did not stop the women. They held more meetings. Soon women across the country began demanding the right to vote. But it would be more than seventy years before American women won the right to vote. Not being able to vote was like a dark cloud hanging over women.

The Civil War slowed down women's fight for the vote. But after the war, women renewed their fight. Two changes to the Constitution made women fight harder. The first change was in 1865. It abolished, or ended, slavery. Many women had fought against slavery. They were happy about this change. The next change was in 1869. It gave all men the right to vote. Men who had been slaves could now vote. But women still could not vote.

Women were angry. They decided to form a new group. Two women, Susan B. Anthony and Elizabeth Cady Stanton, started a group to get women the right to vote. In 1878, Stanton asked Senator Aaron Sargent of California to sponsor a change to the Constitution. This change would allow women to vote. But the change did not pass. Each year, the women tried again. In the meantime, some other women had a different idea about getting women the vote. They wanted each state to give women this right. They thought this was a better way than changing the Constitution. This idea worked in some places.

In 1869, the territory of Wyoming gave women the right to vote. Many pioneer families had settled there. Many women worked and lived there. Wyoming became a state in 1890. It was the first state that allowed women to vote.

Success!

The fight went on. Women tried many things to win the right to vote. In the early 1900s, they held big parades. Some women protested outside the White House. They hoped the president would help them. They marched and carried signs. Some of the women were arrested.

Slowly some people began to listen to the women. They thought about everything that women had done over the years. Women had raised money for their country. Women had helped their country during World War I. Some had worked in factories. Many had joined the armed forces. Some worked in hospitals, helping wounded soldiers. More and more people began to believe that women should be allowed to vote.

Still, the Constitution was not changed. The change was defeated year after year. Finally, in June 1919, the change passed. The Nineteenth Amendment gave women the right to vote. But the fight was not over. Before the change became law, thirty-six states had to

approve it. Women had to fight hard in many states. But in August of 1920, the Nineteenth Amendment became law. Women citizens in the United States finally had the right to vote. Now they could make their voices heard.

Women Get the VOTE

Finding Main Idea and Details

The main idea is the most important idea. The details are the pieces of information that tell more about the main idea.

1. What is the selection mostly about?
   - Ⓐ the Constitution
   - Ⓑ Elizabeth Cady Stanton
   - Ⓒ women winning the right to vote
   - Ⓓ women winning the right to free speech

2. Which of these details was not mentioned in the selection?
   - Ⓐ Many textile mills were in Lowell, Massachusetts.
   - Ⓑ The Constitution was written in 1787.
   - Ⓒ Wyoming was the first state to let women vote.
   - Ⓓ The Nineteenth Amendment gave women the right to vote.

3. Women finally won the right to vote in August of
   - Ⓐ 1800.
   - Ⓑ 1820.
   - Ⓒ 1900.
   - Ⓓ 1920.

Finding Word Meaning in Context

Use context clues to find the meaning of a new word. Context clues are words in a sentence that help you figure out the meaning of the new word.

4. On page 96, what does the word *chores* mean?
   - Ⓐ "unusual household tasks"
   - Ⓑ "regular household tasks"
   - Ⓒ "pieces of furniture"
   - Ⓓ "children's games"

5. Look at page 99. The word *renewed* means
   - Ⓐ "slowed."
   - Ⓑ "stopped again."
   - Ⓒ "started again."
   - Ⓓ "began."

6. On page 99, the word *sponsor* means
   - Ⓐ "support."
   - Ⓑ "rewrite."
   - Ⓒ "advertise."
   - Ⓓ "turn down."

Recognizing Cause and Effect

When one thing causes another thing to happen, it is called cause and effect. The cause is the reason why something happens. The effect is what happens.

7. In the past, some people felt that women should not work because women were too
   - Ⓐ smart.
   - Ⓑ young.
   - Ⓒ strong.
   - Ⓓ weak.

8. In the past, household chores took a long time because women
   - Ⓐ had no timesaving tools.
   - Ⓑ had too many timesaving tools from which to choose.
   - Ⓒ had never learned how to do the chores.
   - Ⓓ spent most of their time away from home.

9. In the 1800s, many women learned how to fight for their own rights as a result of fighting against
   - Ⓐ chores.
   - Ⓑ their husbands.
   - Ⓒ their fathers.
   - Ⓓ slavery.

Comparing and Contrasting

Comparing is finding how two or more things are alike. Contrasting is finding how two or more things are different.

10. In the past, women were often treated like
    - Ⓐ queens.
    - Ⓑ students.
    - Ⓒ servants.
    - Ⓓ soldiers.

11. The author says that not being able to vote was like being under
    - Ⓐ a white cloud.
    - Ⓑ a dark cloud.
    - Ⓒ a rainbow.
    - Ⓓ the ocean.

12. What did Sojourner Truth, Elizabeth Cady Stanton, Lucretia Mott, and Susan B. Anthony have in common?
    - Ⓐ They all spoke out for women's rights.
    - Ⓑ They all spoke out against women's rights.
    - Ⓒ They all lived in Wyoming.
    - Ⓓ They all were former slaves.

Women Get the VOTE

Understanding Sequence

Sequence is the order in which things are done or events happen.

13. Wyoming was the first state to
    Ⓐ have a woman senator.
    Ⓑ end slavery.
    Ⓒ refuse women the right to vote.
    Ⓓ give women the right to vote.

14. According to the selection, where were many women first able to work outside the home?
    Ⓐ in factories
    Ⓑ in textile mills
    Ⓒ in hospitals
    Ⓓ in the White House

15. The boxes show some events related to the right to vote in the United States.

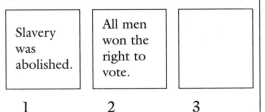

Slavery was abolished.	All men won the right to vote.	
1	2	3

Which of these belongs in box 3?
    Ⓐ Women helped their country during World War I.
    Ⓑ A meeting for women's rights was held at Seneca Falls, New York.
    Ⓒ The Constitution was written.
    Ⓓ All women won the right to vote.

Drawing Conclusions

Drawing conclusions can help you figure out things that are not written in a selection. To draw a conclusion, think about the facts. Then think about what you know in your own life.

16. In the 1700s, what was most highly valued by Americans?
    Ⓐ owning property
    Ⓑ raising children
    Ⓒ keeping house
    Ⓓ being married

17. Senator Aaron Sargent believed that
    Ⓐ women should have the right to vote.
    Ⓑ women should not have the right to vote.
    Ⓒ only individual states should give women the right to vote.
    Ⓓ the Constitution should never be changed.

18. The United States Constitution
    Ⓐ has never been changed.
    Ⓑ can no longer be changed.
    Ⓒ takes time to change.
    Ⓓ can be changed quickly and easily.

Explorations in Writing

Go to page 127.

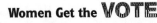

The Growth of the
RAILROAD

Getting Started

Have you ever ridden on a train? Today some trains go more than 150 miles an hour. But the first trains could only go about 20 miles an hour. Passengers were terrified at traveling through the countryside at this great speed! Read this selection to find out more about the railroad in its early days.

GETTING AROUND

In times long past, people got around by walking. They carried things on their back. Then people invented the wheel. With the wheel, people could use carts to carry things. Later, they learned to use horses. They discovered that putting a horse in front of a cart made carrying things even faster and easier. In time, people came up with more and more ideas for improving transportation. The development of the railroad was one of these major advances.

EARLY TRANSPORTATION

Long ago, there were not many roads. And most of the roads were made of dirt. When it rained, the roads turned muddy. Wagon wheels sank into the mud. When the mud dried, deep, hard ruts were left behind. Wagon wheels often broke off in these ruts. More than two thousand years ago, the ancient Greeks put wooden rails on their roads. Wagon wheels moved easily on the rails. This made travel easier. In the mid-1500s, people in Europe and England added wooden rails to their roads. These wooden rails were called "rail-roads." In the 1700s, iron strips were laid over the top of the wooden rails. This kept the rails from wearing out.

Iron rails made the roads easier and safer to use. But horses still pulled the carts that rode along the rails. No one had thought of using machines to pull the carts. Yet for more than a hundred years, steam engines had been around. They were used to pump water out of coal mines.

In 1804, an English inventor, Richard Trevithick, attached a steam engine to a carriage that moved along a track and was able to carry things. Around the same time, an American inventor, Oliver Evans, put a steam engine in a combination boat and wagon. This odd vehicle was designed for digging in rivers, but it could also travel on land. At one point, it traveled through the city streets of Philadelphia, Pennsylvania, at a rate of 3 miles an hour! But it was so heavy, it got stuck in the muddy roads. Still Evans tried to find people to help him build a steam-driven carriage. But most people thought he was crazy.

Early Steam Trains

In 1825, businessman John Stevens built the first steam locomotive in America. He couldn't find people to help him with a big project. But he wanted to try out his idea. So Stevens built a circular track in his backyard and successfully ran the steam locomotive there. That same year in England, a steam locomotive pulled thirty cars loaded with water, coal, flour, and people along an 18-mile track. This train traveled at the terrific speed of 7 or 8 miles an hour.

Five years later in England, the first steam-powered public rail passenger service opened. There were eight cars filled with eight hundred important people. The cars were stagecoaches placed on railroad wheels. This time the train sped along the tracks at up to 29 miles an hour. The passengers thrilled at the speed.

Around the same time, a New York manufacturer, Peter Cooper, built a little steam locomotive. It became known as the *Tom Thumb*. On its first trip, the locomotive was challenged to a race by

The Tom Thumb *is winning at this point in the race.*

a horse-drawn railcar. The horse quickly took the lead. But the *Tom Thumb* gained speed and passed it. The race seemed to be won. The driver of the horse was about to give up. Then suddenly a part of the locomotive broke. The engine began to slow. The horse won! Nevertheless, people became convinced that the railroad would soon replace the horse.

INVENTIONS There were many problems to solve with the early railroads. People thought that a locomotive could never pull a train uphill. They believed that the wheels would just spin around and around on the tracks. So the first railroad tracks were laid only on flat ground. But then railroad builders tried laying tracks up hills. They discovered that a locomotive could pull a train uphill after all.

People also wondered if trains could run in snow. Wouldn't snow block the tracks? People solved this problem by attaching a V-shaped metal plate to the front of the locomotive. The locomotive then became a kind of snowplow. It pushed the snow out of the way.

Many trains ran through farm country. And trains sometimes killed animals that were crossing the tracks at the wrong time. This could also knock the train off the track. To solve this problem, someone invented a cowcatcher. The metal cowcatcher was attached to the front of the engine. The cowcatcher pushed animals off the tracks.

At first, trains ran only in the daytime. This was because the engineers couldn't see the tracks at night. Then someone invented the headlight. It was a candle set inside a glass protector. This kept the wind from blowing the flame out. Later headlamps used the fuel kerosene. This gave out a much stronger light. In the 1880s, someone invented an electric headlight, which gave out the best light of all.

Sometimes rails became very slippery from ice or other problems. In 1836, Pennsylvania had a great grasshopper plague. Squashed grasshoppers made the tracks so slick that a locomotive could barely move. Its wheels just spun in place. At last, one of the crew jumped out and shoveled sand onto the rails. It worked! The train moved forward. After that, train crews carried sand with them to use on wet or icy tracks.

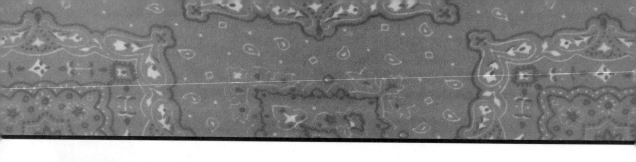

farms and clean air. Trains were noisy. Their engines gave out sparks that sometimes started fires beside the tracks. Smoke stained the air. Trains scared or even killed livestock.

Yet trains also brought growth. Towns grew up around the railroad because trains brought business. People used trains to ship and receive goods. Inns that had once served stagecoaches soon became railroad stations. For the first time, people could travel longer distances easily. They could visit friends and relatives.

The railroad also created an interesting separation. Towns through which trains traveled developed a "right" side and a "wrong" side of the tracks. The wind usually blew the trains' black smoke in the same direction, over to the "wrong" side of the tracks. This became the low rent side. This was where the poor lived and where factories were built. The "right" side was where those with more money lived and where expensive shops were built.

CHANGES People began to believe that the railroad was the way of the future. Rail lines were built throughout the eastern part of the United States. Whenever a new stretch of track was completed, people came from miles around to celebrate.

Not everyone was happy about the arrival of the railroad, though. At that time, most of America was a land of quiet

DANGERS Train rides were exciting. But they weren't always very safe. People who lived along the tracks watched for things that could cause problems for the trains. After storms, they checked to see if any tracks or railroad bridges had been damaged. If they found a problem, they ran toward an oncoming train. They waved something bright at the engineer to stop him. Bright red underwear was in fashion then. Often that was what people waved. Red became known as the color for danger. Red flags and red lights became railroad danger signals.

Early rails were not very strong. Passing trains sometimes loosened them. The metal strips could then curl up and burst through the railroad car floor. Sometimes passengers were hurt. These metal strips were called "snakeheads." They were as dangerous as snakes.

The first trains had many accidents. The trains moved very slowly, though. So the accidents were rarely serious. But by the 1850s, some accidents were terrible disasters. The first took place in 1853. The engineer of a train traveling from New York to Boston crossed the Norwalk River. He didn't notice the signal telling him the drawbridge was open. The locomotive, three passenger cars, and the baggage car fell into the river. Forty-six people died. Eighty others were injured. After this accident, people demanded better safety rules for the railroad.

COMFORT   In the early days of train travel, passengers were not always comfortable. First-class passengers sat behind glass windows. But second-class passengers sat by open windows. And third-class passengers rode in open cars, with no roofs. Black soot and hot cinders from the locomotive fell onto them.

The early cars were unheated. Then stoves were added to one end of each car. But this meant that passengers were either very hot or very cold. Trains had no restaurant cars. Passengers had to bring food along or buy food at stops along the way. The price and the quality of the food varied a lot.

In 1864, George Pullman developed a better passenger car. It was called the Pullman car. This car had comfortable padded seats and pull-down beds. In the 1870s, Pullman added dining cars.

A Pullman Car

Wealthy passengers could sit down to good meals in elegant cars. The poor, however, continued to travel in discomfort. Their cars jerked and bounced along. The crowded passengers sat on hard, straight-backed benches. They slept on these benches. Or they slept on the floor. Though early train travel was hard for some, most considered traveling by train a great adventure.

Finding Main Idea and Details

The main idea is the most important idea. The details are the pieces of information that tell more about the main idea.

1. What is the selection mostly about?
   - Ⓐ the early railroad
   - Ⓑ today's trains
   - Ⓒ inventions
   - Ⓓ disasters

2. Which of these details about trains was not mentioned in the selection?
   - Ⓐ The first Pullman cars had pull-down beds.
   - Ⓑ In 1837, steam whistles were added to locomotives.
   - Ⓒ The ancient Greeks put wooden rails on their roads.
   - Ⓓ Sand helps trains move on wet or icy tracks.

3. Who built the first steam locomotive in America?
   - Ⓐ Tom Thumb
   - Ⓑ Peter Cooper
   - Ⓒ John Stevens
   - Ⓓ George Pullman

Finding Word Meaning in Context

Use context clues to find the meaning of a new word. Context clues are words in a sentence that help you figure out the meaning of the new word.

4. On page 105, the word *ruts* means
   - Ⓐ "flat roads."
   - Ⓑ "steep hills."
   - Ⓒ "deep, narrow tracks."
   - Ⓓ "huge ditches."

5. On page 105, a *vehicle* is something that you
   - Ⓐ carry.
   - Ⓑ talk to.
   - Ⓒ listen to.
   - Ⓓ ride in.

6. Look at page 109. Which word best describes *disasters*?
   - Ⓐ troublesome
   - Ⓑ average
   - Ⓒ horrible
   - Ⓓ upsetting

Recognizing Cause and Effect

When one thing causes another thing to happen, it is called cause and effect. The cause is the reason why something happens. The effect is what happens.

7. Iron strips were laid over wooden rails to
   Ⓐ keep them from wearing out.
   Ⓑ keep them from getting wet.
   Ⓒ cut down on noise.
   Ⓓ cut down on cost.

8. The horse-drawn railcar beat the *Tom Thumb* because
   Ⓐ the horse was faster.
   Ⓑ a part of the locomotive broke.
   Ⓒ an animal wandered onto the tracks.
   Ⓓ the locomotive was faster.

9. Train crews brought sand along with them to be prepared for
   Ⓐ cows.
   Ⓑ earthquakes.
   Ⓒ fire.
   Ⓓ ice.

Comparing and Contrasting

Comparing is finding how two or more things are alike. Contrasting is finding how two or more things are different.

10. Expensive shops were built on the "right" side of the tracks, but what was built on the "wrong" side of the tracks?
    Ⓐ fine homes
    Ⓑ railroad stations
    Ⓒ factories
    Ⓓ inns

11. On the earliest trains, what did first-class and second-class passengers have that third-class passengers did not have?
    Ⓐ a roof over their head
    Ⓑ a wooden floor
    Ⓒ padded seats
    Ⓓ glass windows

12. Loosened metal rails that burst through train floors were compared to
    Ⓐ roads.
    Ⓑ horses.
    Ⓒ grasshoppers.
    Ⓓ snakes.

THE GROWTH OF THE RAILROAD

Understanding Sequence

Sequence is the order in which things are done or events happen.

13. The boxes tell about the development of the railroad.

John Stevens built the first steam locomotive in America.		The first train disaster took place.
1	2	3

Which of these belongs in box 2?

Ⓐ Iron strips were laid over wooden rails.

Ⓑ The first steam-powered rail passenger service opened.

Ⓒ The Greeks put wooden rails on their roads.

Ⓓ George Pullman developed the Pullman car.

14. Which was the most recent power source used to light train headlamps?

Ⓐ electricity

Ⓑ candles

Ⓒ wood

Ⓓ kerosene

15. If people found a problem on a railroad bridge, they

Ⓐ didn't tell anyone else about it.

Ⓑ poured sand on the tracks.

Ⓒ pulled up the drawbridge.

Ⓓ waved to warn the engineer.

Drawing Conclusions

Drawing conclusions can help you figure out things that are not written in a selection. To draw a conclusion, think about the facts. Then think about what you know in your own life.

16. In 1804, the streets of Philadelphia on which Oliver Evans drove his vehicle probably had

Ⓐ wooden rails.

Ⓑ iron rails.

Ⓒ no rails.

Ⓓ concrete paving.

17. From this selection, you can tell that people usually invent things to

Ⓐ get rich.

Ⓑ solve problems.

Ⓒ win contests.

Ⓓ win praise.

18. Early train travel was much more comfortable if you were

Ⓐ rich.

Ⓑ young.

Ⓒ adventurous.

Ⓓ a member of the crew.

Explorations in Writing

Go to page 128.

A TOUR OF JAPAN

GETTING STARTED

Have you ever wanted to visit Japan? You could see beautiful Mount Fuji. Or you could visit the cities of Tokyo and Hagi. Sit back and take a mini-tour of Japan in this selection.

THE LAND

Japan is an island country located in the Pacific Ocean, off the eastern coast of Asia. It is near Russia, Korea, and China. Japan is made up of four large islands, dozens of smaller islands, and thousands of tiny islets. A volcano formed these islands long ago. If you put Japan over a map of the United States, Japan would stretch from Bangor, Maine, in the north to Jacksonville, Florida, in the south. The northern part of Japan is sometimes cold enough for snow. The southern part of Japan stays warm.

Much of Japan is covered with mountains. Few people can live on the mountains, though. Most people live on the plains between the mountains. Almost thirty million people live in and around the capital city of Tokyo.

An old Japanese tale tells how the gods made the land of Japan long ago. They made Japan beautiful. They made high mountains covered with snow. The mountains were a special blue color. The gods made beautiful lakes and rivers, too. Nature in Japan was like a picture come-to-life. Japan was so beautiful that the gods decided to live there.

Today the Japanese still love nature. It is very important to them. A Japanese saying is "to be one with nature." One of the most beautiful natural sights in the world, Mount Fuji, is in Japan.

MOUNT FUJI

Mount Fuji is the highest peak in Japan. It is part of a chain of volcanoes located near the center of Japan. Mount Fuji was formed over five thousand years ago. It is 12,386 feet tall. Mount Fuji has erupted several times. The last time was in 1707. For almost three hundred years, it has been silent. Some scientists warn that Mount Fuji may erupt again soon. But no one can say exactly when.

The Japanese people have admired cone-shaped Mount Fuji for a long time. Many people visit this beautiful mountain. Pictures of it appear in almost all of Japan's tourist booklets. Poets write about Mount Fuji. Painters often paint it. One famous painter, Katshushika Hokusai, created thirty-six different views of the mountain. His paintings are famous all over the world.

Mount Fuji

HOT SPRINGS

Japan is also known for its hot springs. People have been coming to these springs for over eight hundred years. Many people travel to the springs to bathe. The hot water is said to make people feel better. One of the most famous hot springs is at Kusatsu. There the hot springs flow out at almost ten thousand gallons per minute. The water from these springs is said to help cure skin diseases.

116

CITIES

Many people visit Tokyo, Japan's capital. Tokyo is a very busy city. It is always full of people. The streets are crowded and noisy. To get

around the city, many people ride bikes. This is often faster than driving a car. Many people visit the Imperial Palace. This is the home of the emperor, the ruler of Japan. People cannot go inside the palace. They can visit the gardens around it, though.

Tokyo has many restaurants and shops. Many restaurants serve traditional Japanese dishes. One favorite dish in Japan is noodle soup. There are many kinds of noodle soup. People eat the soup with fish, beef, shrimp, or eel. Eel is a special treat in Japan.

Tokyo at Night

Tokyo is a modern city. But when people want to see a very old town, they often go to Hagi. Visiting Hagi is like stepping back in time. Most ancient Japanese cities have been modernized. Hagi has not. It has many rare and very old houses. The houses have dark gray tile roofs and white walls. Hagi was built around its ruler's castle. Long ago, warriors protected the rich merchants and the local ruler. These warriors were called samurai. Visitors today can see the homes of the merchants and the samurai.

People also visit Usuki City. They go there to see the famous stone Buddhas. Buddha was a religious leader in Asia. Many Japanese people follow this religion. The stone Buddhas were carved six to eight hundred years ago. Some were carved into the sides of rock faces on hillsides. Others were carved from loose rocks. The stone used to carve the statues was soft. Over time, weather has damaged them. Today, many of the Buddhas have been restored.

A Stone Buddha

FESTIVALS

Japan has many different festivals. One of the most beautiful is the kite festival. Here people fly large, beautiful kites. At doll festivals, people make and exchange dolls. Most of the festivals have music and dancing. There may also be special food and clothing.

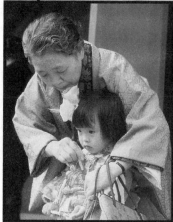

A little girl and her grandmother get ready for a festival.

One popular festival is the Sapporo Snow Festival. This festival began in 1950. It takes place in mid-February every year. For seven days, people make and display hundreds of snow statues and ice sculptures. Local high school students started this festival. One day, they made six snow statues in the local park. Many people stopped to look at the statues. The students made snow statues again the next year. Each year, the festival grew larger. Now more than two million people come to the festival each year.

Another special festival is the Nebuta Festival. It has a parade of huge lanterns in the shape of samurai. The lanterns have wooden or bamboo frames. They are covered with brightly colored papier-mâché. Some of the lanterns are as high as twenty-six feet and as wide as forty-nine feet. Even children carry small lanterns. The lanterns are lit at dusk. The large

The Nebuta Festival

lanterns are put on floats. Many people pull each float along. The festival is like the big Thanksgiving Day Parade in New York City. Judges vote for the three best floats. The winners are put on boats that sail around for all to see.

THE ARTS

Japan is famous for its arts. Many of these arts have been practiced for hundreds of years.

DOLLS People around the world admire Japanese dolls. Two of the most famous are the Hakata doll and the Iwatsuki doll. Each kind of doll has its own style. The lovely Hakata dolls are pottery. They are made from clay that has been carved. They are known for their smooth white skin. The dolls' skin looks almost transparent. One artist paints each doll. Sometimes a doll is dressed to look like the person who is buying it.

The Iwatsuki dolls are wooden. They are made from sawdust that has been kneaded into solid form. These dolls are made in Iwatsuki City, known as "Doll City." This city has more than three hundred doll workshops and one hundred doll stores. There are special dolls for boys and girls. Parents often buy these dolls for their children as a sign of good health.

Japanese dolls are admired around the world.

POETRY Haiku (HIGH coo) is a special kind of Japanese poetry. A haiku has three lines. The first line has five syllables. The second line has seven syllables. The third line has five syllables. Haiku is usually about nature. Poets began writing haiku over four hundred years ago. Issa was a famous haiku poet in Japan. Today many people study his poems. The poem to the right is a haiku.

> the mountain soars high
> wearing a deep purple coat
> and a crown of white

THEATER Japan is famous for two special kinds of theater. One is Kabuki theater. A woman named Okuni started it in the 1600s. She danced and sang. Over the next three hundred years, actors developed it. Kabuki theater has a unique style. The plays are about events in history or everyday life. The actors paint their faces white. They wear special make-up for their roles. Colors are very important in Kabuki theater. The colors tell whether the characters are good or evil. Even though a woman started this kind of theater, the roles today are all played by men. Kabuki actors are very famous in Japan.

Theater is important in Japan.

Noh is another special kind of Japanese theater. It is mostly dance. The dancers perform their movements very slowly. Noh actors wear masks. Masks are very important. They show the actors' emotions. There are more than two hundred kinds of Noh masks. Today many of the masks from ancient times are in museums.

JAPAN TODAY

Japan is known for its ancient arts. But modern Japan is also known for its computers and electronic games and other electronic products. Japan today offers a look back to the past. It also offers a look forward to the future.

Japan Today

A TOUR OF JAPAN

Finding Main Idea and Details

The main idea is the most important idea. The details are the pieces of information that tell more about the main idea.

1. Which of these details about Japan was not mentioned in the selection?
   - Ⓐ Usuki City is famous for its stone Buddhas.
   - Ⓑ The New Year's Festival is the biggest festival in Japan.
   - Ⓒ The Imperial Palace is the home of the emperor.
   - Ⓓ Tokyo is the capital of Japan.

2. Page 117 is mostly about
   - Ⓐ transportation in Tokyo.
   - Ⓑ different kinds of noodle soup.
   - Ⓒ cities in Japan.
   - Ⓓ castles in Japan.

3. How many gallons of water flow out each minute in Kusatsu?
   - Ⓐ ten thousand
   - Ⓑ one thousand
   - Ⓒ one hundred
   - Ⓓ one hundred thousand

Finding Word Meaning in Context

Use context clues to find the meaning of a new word. Context clues are words in a sentence that help you figure out the meaning of the new word.

4. Look at page 115. *Islets* are very tiny
   - Ⓐ rivers.
   - Ⓑ lakes.
   - Ⓒ islands.
   - Ⓓ mountains.

5. On page 116, *erupted* means
   - Ⓐ "disappeared."
   - Ⓑ "blown away."
   - Ⓒ "shot material out suddenly."
   - Ⓓ "leaked material out slowly."

6. Look at page 117. When something is *restored*, what is done to it?
   - Ⓐ It is broken.
   - Ⓑ It is purchased.
   - Ⓒ It is returned.
   - Ⓓ It is fixed.

Recognizing Cause and Effect

When one thing causes another thing to happen, it is called cause and effect. The cause is the reason why something happens. The effect is what happens.

7. People travel to the hot springs to
    Ⓐ   be cured.
    Ⓑ   be entertained.
    Ⓒ   swim.
    Ⓓ   meet new friends.

8. According to the selection, many people ride bikes around the city of Tokyo because riding a bike is
    Ⓐ   slower than driving a car.
    Ⓑ   better exercise than driving a car.
    Ⓒ   more fun than driving a car.
    Ⓓ   faster than driving a car.

9. Many stone Buddhas have been damaged by
    Ⓐ   visitors.
    Ⓑ   weather.
    Ⓒ   volcanoes.
    Ⓓ   thieves.

Comparing and Contrasting

Comparing is finding how two or more things are alike. Contrasting is finding how two or more things are different.

10. Unlike most Japanese cities, Hagi has not been
    Ⓐ   modernized.
    Ⓑ   cleaned.
    Ⓒ   lived in.
    Ⓓ   visited by tourists.

11. Hakata dolls are made from pottery, but Iwatsuki dolls are made from
    Ⓐ   stone.
    Ⓑ   sawdust.
    Ⓒ   clay.
    Ⓓ   yarn.

12. Noh theater is different from Kabuki theater in that Noh actors all use
    Ⓐ   make-up.
    Ⓑ   swords.
    Ⓒ   wigs.
    Ⓓ   masks.

A TOUR OF JAPAN

Understanding Sequence

Sequence is the order in which things are done or events happen.

13. According to the old Japanese tale, what did the gods decide to do after they had completed Japan?
    Ⓐ make another country
    Ⓑ make more lakes and rivers
    Ⓒ live in Japan
    Ⓓ live in China

14. Mount Fuji last erupted in
    Ⓐ 1607.
    Ⓑ 1707.
    Ⓒ 1807.
    Ⓓ 1907.

15. The last line of a haiku has how many syllables?
    Ⓐ seven
    Ⓑ four
    Ⓒ three
    Ⓓ five

Drawing Conclusions

Drawing conclusions can help you figure out things that are not written in a selection. To draw a conclusion, think about the facts. Then think about what you know in your own life.

16. During a visit to Japan, you would probably not see any
    Ⓐ oceans.
    Ⓑ mountains.
    Ⓒ deserts.
    Ⓓ rivers.

17. According to the selection, which word best describes the samurai?
    Ⓐ artistic
    Ⓑ comical
    Ⓒ cruel
    Ⓓ powerful

18. Sapporo is in
    Ⓐ northern Japan.
    Ⓑ southern Japan.
    Ⓒ Nebuta.
    Ⓓ Korea.

Explorations in Writing

Go to page 128.

Explorations in Writing

Write your answers on a separate piece of paper.

Wolf! (pages 4–10)

1. The author gives a lot of information about wolves. Write some things that you have learned about wolves.

2. Look at the photos of the German shepherd and the Alaskan husky on page 5. Then look at the photos of wolves in the rest of the selection. Use your own words to tell how dogs and wolves look alike.

3. Read again the section called "Pack Life" on page 8. Tell what the pack means to wolves.

THE WILD WEST SHOW (pages 14–20)

1. The author tells about "Buffalo Bill" Cody. Write about something interesting in Cody's life.

2. A fact can be proved. An opinion is what someone thinks or feels.
   - Here is a fact from the selection: Lewis and Clark explored the West.
   - Here is an opinion based on the selection: Annie Oakley was the best sharpshooter in the world.

   Write three more facts from the selection. Write at least one more opinion based on the selection. Give a reason for each of your opinions.

3. Write about why Sitting Bull stayed with the Wild West Show for just one year.

TIDE POOLS (pages 24–30)

1. The author gives a lot of information about tide pools. Write about one kind of animal that lives in a tide pool.

2. Look at the sea anemones on page 29. Describe what a sea anemone looks like.

3. A tide pool is a hard place in which to live. In your own words, tell why life is difficult for animals living in a tide pool.

Explorations in Writing

Explorations in Writing

Write your answers on a separate piece of paper.

GROWING UP IN ANCIENT GREECE
(pages 34–40)

1. The author tells about life in ancient Greece. Write about one part of life in ancient Greece—play, school, or work, for example.

2. A fact can be proved. An opinion is what someone thinks or feels.
   - Here is a fact from the selection: Ancient Greece was made up of city-states.
   - Here is an opinion based on the selection: Ancient Greece was a wonderful place in which to live and learn.

   Write three more facts from the selection. Write one or two more opinions based on the selection. Give a reason for each of your opinions.

3. Ancient Greece contributed many things to the world today. Write about a few of these things.

Migration
(pages 44–50)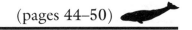

1. The author tells about different ways that animals migrate. Write about how one kind of animal migrates.

2. Look at page 46. The map shows the migratory route of gray whales. In your own words, describe the whales' journey.

3. The author says that animals migrate for various reasons. In your own words, tell why some animals migrate.

Explorations in Writing

Write your answers on a separate piece of paper.

Benjamin Franklin

(pages 54–60)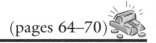

1. The author gives a lot of information about Benjamin Franklin. Describe the kind of man you think Franklin was.

2. A fact can be proved. An opinion is what someone thinks or feels.
   - Here is a fact from the selection: Franklin was born in Boston.
   - Here is an opinion based on the selection: Franklin was a very clever man.

   Write three more facts from the selection. Write one or two more opinions based on the selection. Give a reason for each of your opinions.

3. In your opinion, what was Franklin's most important contribution to his country? Write about it.

It's GOLD!

(pages 64–70)

1. The author tells why many people think gold is important. Write about why you think gold is or is not important.

2. A fact can be proved. An opinion is what someone thinks or feels.
   - Here is a fact from the selection: One gold nugget weighed 195 pounds.
   - Here is an opinion based on the selection: Gold is the most beautiful metal in the world.

   Write three more facts from the selection. Write one or two more opinions based on the selection. Give a reason for each of your opinions.

3. Write about some of the ways in which gold was used by people long ago.

Explorations in Writing

Explorations in Writing

Write your answers on a separate piece of paper.

LANGSTON HUGHES, *the Original Jazz Poet* (pages 74–80)

1. The author tells about the early life of Langston Hughes. Use your own words to tell what Langston's early life was like.

2. On page 80, the author says that Hughes was used to *living hand-to-mouth*. In your own words, tell what this means.

3. The author tells how Hughes traveled the country reading his poetry. Why was this was a good way for Hughes to make money? Write about it.

The OLYMPIC GAMES, Then and Now (pages 84–90)

1. The author tells about the first Olympic Games. Write about these early games in your own words.

2. Look at the illustration on page 84. How does it make you feel? Tell what it might be like to be in the Olympics.

3. The author describes different events in both the Summer Games and the Winter Games. Write about a few of the events.

Women Get the VOTE (pages 94–100)

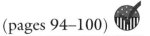

1. The author tells how women got the right to vote. Write about how women accomplished this goal.

2. On page 96, the author says that women were *treated like servants*. In your own words, tell what this means.

3. Read page 98 again. The meeting in Seneca Falls was very important for women. Write about why this meeting was so important.

Explorations in Writing

Explorations in Writing

Write your answers on a separate piece of paper.

THE GROWTH OF THE RAILROAD   (pages 104–110)

1. The author tells a lot about the early railroad. Write about why the early railroad was important and how it changed the way people lived.

2. On page 108, the author says that *smoke stained the air*. Describe this in your own words.

3. Different kinds of passengers had different kinds of experiences riding early trains. Write about what it was like to ride in a third-class car. Or write what it was like to ride in a Pullman car.

A TOUR OF JAPAN   (pages 114–120)

1. In this selection, the author gives a lot of information about Japan. If you visited Japan, what would you see and do? Write about your trip to Japan.

2. Read again the haiku on page 119. What images does the haiku create in your mind? Use your own words to describe the images.

3. Japan is a land of mountains. Read again the section on page 116 about Mount Fuji. Write about this beautiful mountain.

Explorations in Writing